PENGUIN BOOKS

EVERYDAY PARENTING

Robin Goldstein, M.A., is a parenting consultant and educator who has had many years of experience working with young children and their families. She has taught college courses on child development and helps preschools plan and improve their programs. In addition, she writes a newspaper column on child rearing. She wrote *Everyday Parenting* to answer the questions that parents most often ask her. Robin Goldstein and her husband and two children live in Maryland.

EVERYDAY PARENTING

The First Five Years

Robin Goldstein

with Janet Gallant

PENGUIN BOOKS

PENGUIN BOOKS
Published by the Penguin Group
Penguin Books USA Inc.,
375 Hudson Street, New York, New York 10014, U.S.A.
Penguin Books Ltd, 27 Wrights Lane,
London W8 5TZ, England
Penguin Books Australia Ltd, Ringwood,
Victoria, Australia
Penguin Books Canada Ltd, 10 Alcorn Avenue,
Toronto, Ontario, Canada M4V 3B2
Penguin Books (N.Z.) Ltd, 182–190 Wairau Road,
Auckland 10, New Zealand

Penguin Books Ltd, Registered Offices:
Harmondsworth, Middlesex, England

First published in the United States of America by AriAnna Press 1987
This revised edition published in Penguin Books 1990

10 9 8 7 6 5 4

Illustration credits appear on page ix.

Coke is a registered trademark of the Coca Cola Company.
Band-Aid is a registered trademark of Johnson & Johnson.

LIBRARY OF CONGRESS CATALOGING IN PUBLICATION DATA
Goldstein, Robin.
Everyday parenting: the first five years / Robin Goldstein.
p. cm.
Reprint. Originally published: Rockville, Md.: AriAnna Press,
1987.
ISBN 0 14 01.3345 3
1. Toddlers. 2. Preschool children. 3. Child rearing.
I. Title.
HQ774.5.G65 1990
649′.1—dc20   89-48027

Printed in the United States of America
Set in Times Roman
Designed by Bernard Schleifer

Dedicated to my husband,
my children, and my parents.

Acknowledgments

I wrote this book with the help and encouragement of my family and friends. Thanks to my husband, Miles, who gave constant support, read and re-read the manuscript and offered fresh ideas and insights; to Janet Gallant, who gave friendship, help and guidance; to Alice Fins, who was a consistent source of support; to Linda Elliot, who patiently helped with typing; and most important, to my children, Ari and Anna, who taught me so much about the importance of trusting and respecting children.

About the Illustrations

All the artwork in this book was done by children. Their drawings, aside from being spontaneous and wonderful to look at, help to show adults what the world is like from a child's point of view. A special thank you to all the artists:

Brian Dubin
Jason Dubin
Toby Dubin
Danny Gallant
Michael Gallant
Anna Goldstein
Ari Goldstein
Michelle Litman
Rachel Litman
Keri Orgel
Todd Orgel

Contents

Sleeping

Eating

Independence

Setting Limits

Children's Thinking

Fears and Imagination

Toys, Play, and Socializing

Being Nice

Caretakers and Preschools

Introduction

"Should I pick my baby up when he cries?"

"What can I do if my child has a temper tantrum in the grocery store?"

"Why is my 4-year-old still attached to her blanket?"

"Why doesn't my child listen to me?"

These questions reflect the everyday issues of parenting—the practical problems faced by all parents of children 5 years old and under. Raising young children is a difficult job, often made harder by the isolation many contemporary parents feel. In our society, most traditional sources of advice and support, such as the extended family, are no longer available. And parents, who feel pressure to be self-sufficient and produce exceptional children, are often unwilling to talk to others about child rearing problems. *Everyday Parenting* is designed to help modern families by filling the "support gap" and providing reassurance, useable information on child development, and concrete advice.

When parents are unaware of what other families are going through, they may feel their own problems are unique. Parents wonder, "Is my child the only 18-month-old not sleeping through the night?" "Do other parents have to repeat and repeat before their children listen?" "Is something wrong with my child?" *Everyday Parenting* reassures parents by letting them know that most families with young children go through similar struggles and experiences. Also, by describing children's thinking (based on the work of Jean Piaget) and the predictable stages of child development, this book lets parents know that most of their children's behavior is completely normal. Parents need a basic understanding of child development in order to form realistic expectations.

Unrealistic expectations, usually based on inadequate information, cause many struggles between parents and children. A father who is upset because his 9-month-old shies away from strangers, and a mother who is concerned because her 2-year-old is not interested in using the toilet, may not understand their children's developmental needs and stages. Both these children are exhibiting normal behavior for their ages. Once parents learn what kind of behavior to expect from their children, they will no longer face the conflicts that come from anticipating that, for example, a 3-year-old will behave as a 4- or 5-year-old would.

Everyday Parenting offers a great deal of practical, sensible advice for dealing with everyday problems. Too often parents are given advice that shows no understanding of children's real needs and growth patterns. Parents are urged to take things away from children (bottle, breast, blanket, etc.) and to force children to do things (separate from parents, share toys, learn the ABCs, etc.) before the children and their parents are ready. This kind of pressuring advice leads parents to doubt their own instincts or to hide what they do in order to avoid ridicule. But the advice in *Everyday Parenting* is offered with a sense of respect for parents and children and is based solidly on the chronology of child development. A range of options is presented so parents can follow the suggestions that seem most appropriate.

The book is arranged by major issues, with a separate article for each specific concern. Articles grouped together deal with related topics, but each article is self-contained so parents can begin anywhere and use the book as a quick reference and source of help. Most articles start with a general discussion of the issue and then move, when appropriate, to specific suggestions for parents. In some instances, much space is devoted to a seemingly minor problem such as young children's fear of Santa Claus, while a more global subject such as separation anxiety receives less attention. This happens because *Everyday Parenting* offers practical advice on the specific issues of child rearing, and does not attempt a comprehensive look at theory. There are excellent books available for parents who wish to learn more about development.

The articles deal with the period from infancy to 5 years of age. Throughout the book, wide age ranges are given for most specific behaviors because normal children develop at different rates: one child may sleep through the night at 3 months while another may not be ready until age 2 or even 3. The advice given applies to children 5 and under, and is not intended to be used for older children. What is appropriate for parents to do with a 2- or 3-year-old is often inappropriate when a child over 5 is involved.

Each article deals with one sex, and the sexes are alternated so that an article about "him" is followed by an article about "her." This was done to include both sexes equally, but all the information applies to all children. Similarly, although the articles generally speak of parents dealing with one child, the advice is, of course, applicable to families with any number of children.

The day-to-day issues of childrearing are very important. It is parents' responses to everyday situations that ultimately shape the psychological foundations of their children's lives. In order to help their children feel good about themselves and the world, parents have to respond to their children's needs with an understanding of social, emotional, intellectual, and physical development. This difficult job, which requires an enormous amount of love, time, and attention, is one for which parents deserve support. *Everyday Parenting* acknowledges the frustrations and uncertainty of raising children and offers parents encouragement. With the help provided by the information and suggestions in this book, parenting can be an easier and more enjoyable job.

DEPENDENCY

Is My Child Too Dependent on Me?

Expectant parents often fantasize about the pleasure their child will give them. But when the baby arrives, new parents discover that they are the ones who must initially do most of the giving. Many parents are surprised at how much time, attention, and effort child care involves. And some parents are dismayed to learn how many of their own needs they have to give up in order to care for their child. In spite of all the joy a new baby brings, parenting at first can feel like an unequal proposition—parents give while the baby receives.

When parents discover how naturally demanding and dependent their baby is, they sometimes worry about "giving in" to all his needs. If they pick him up when he cries, offer a bottle or breast on demand, or keep him with them through the day, will he soon become too dependent on them? In our society, independence is viewed as a positive trait and many parents become concerned if their babies seem too attached to people or objects.

Some adults feel that it is never too soon to start teaching a child to become independent. "He's going to have to learn sometime that he can't always have his way." "He's going to have to learn what life is really like." And some people also believe that giving in to a child's needs in infancy will make it that much harder to get the child to give up his dependencies later on.

Parents who are uneasy about how dependent their young child is may, in an attempt to foster independence, make conscious decisions not to meet all of his needs. They may hesitate to pick him up when he cries, or they may hold back on cuddling or frequent nursing. They may feel guilty and full of self-doubt whenever they do give more than they think they should. Yet when parents fully understand their child's dependency needs, they see that there is no need to worry about a baby's lack of self-sufficiency.

Infants and young children are almost totally dependent on adults; this is a natural and necessary condition of early childhood. It is normal for babies to want the constant comfort of being cared for, held, fed, changed, loved, and played with, and there is nothing harmful about giving to a young child. A child whose needs are met and who has a strong attachment to his parents will develop a foundation of trust that will allow him to gradually become independent.

If your baby learns to trust your care and support, he will grow into a toddler who explores his surroundings with confidence. And as he grows, his natural drive for independence will begin to show. The 10-month-old will want to feed himself, the 2-year-old will cry out, "I'll do it myself," the 3-year-old will feel independent going off on his tricycle, and the 5-year-old will want to spend long periods of time with his friends.

Your young child will always have a strong need to be cared for, of course, but as he gets older, he will become more and more independent, and you will spend less time giving. And although there will be times in your child's life when he will temporarily become more dependent—when he enters pre-school, when the family moves, when a sibling is born, etc.— if his early dependency needs have been met he will move into the world with a greater sense of confidence.

4

Should I Pick My Baby Up When She Cries?

Crying is a baby's way of communicating. Particularly in the early months, a child cries when she is hungry, cold, wet, tired, and when she wants to be held and played with. She knows the world as either pleasurable or uncomfortable; when her needs are met she feels good, and when they aren't she feels bad and cries.

Many parents wonder how they should respond when their child cries. If they pick her up each time, will her demands increase? And is there a chance she will become spoiled? Parents who wish to follow their instincts and respond to their child's tears are often confused by people who say, "Don't pick her up, you'll spoil her," "Let her cry, it's good for her lungs," or "You can't always be there for her."

The truth is that picking up a crying baby won't spoil her. Rather, it will help her develop a sense of security that will actually make her less likely to cry in the long run. Babies whose cries bring a helpful response begin to anticipate that whenever they cry, someone will respond. This cause-and-effect connection gives the child a secure and comfortable feeling and also teaches her to trust her parents. And learning to trust is a critical part of early development. If the adults caring for a baby do not respond to her cries, or respond erratically and unpredictably, the child will quickly sense that there is little she can do to affect her environment. In such a situation, she will learn to mistrust those around her.

Of course, there is a wide range of possible parental behavior between the extremes of total responsiveness and unresponsiveness. No matter how hard parents try to calm and comfort their child, there will be times when she remains frustrated. But if parents are consistently caring during the early months, their child will start life with a sense of trust.

Comforting a crying child is very important, but it can also be difficult, especially if the child cries often, or during a busy moment. If you find that your baby needs a lot of comforting during the day, you may want to try a cloth infant carrier that will let you hold her close while leaving your hands free. The contact and constant movement can be very soothing to a child.

If your baby does a lot of crying at night, you may feel frustrated and unsure about how to respond. Your natural instinct may be to pick her up, but you also may be tired, and you may be getting negative advice. Your pediatrician might advise you to let your child "cry it out at night," particularly once she turns 3-months-old. Many people advocate ignoring a child's cries in the hope that she will learn to sleep through the night. One theory states that if parents refuse to comfort or feed their child during the night, she will stop crying after 20 minutes to one hour and go back to sleep. After many days or weeks of this routine the child will no longer wake up at night.

Although the prospect of an evening of uninterrupted sleep may certainly be attractive to you, it is better not to let your child cry during the night. When you get up and comfort her, you let her know that she can depend on you, that she is worthwhile, and that you care about meeting her needs. Holding her and soothing her, you give her a sense of security and a basis for developing trust in her world.

Is My Baby "Good"?

Is a "good" baby one who sleeps a lot and doesn't cry much? Most people say "yes," and their answer is understandable. "Good" and "bad" are judgmental terms people often use to describe the behavior and temperament of a baby. A "good" baby is a quiet one; a "bad" baby is a fussy one.

Labeling babies begins very early. One new mother was told by a maternity nurse that her hungry infant had been crying in the nursery. "What a bad baby you have!" Parents often experience such labeling when they are out in public: a well-meaning person will approach a mother and infant and say, "What a good baby. Is he always like this?" A question like this can put the mother in a bind. Although she may answer "yes," she may also remember that the previous week he had cried all during a shopping trip.

Parents often feel judged and may believe that their child is a reflection on them. Every parent wants a contented child who is easy to care for because such a baby gives his parents a feeling of success. And many parents feel bad if their baby cries or has colic. Yet the fussing baby is not "bad" and the quiet baby is not "good." All babies are different. Labeling and judging them for their behavior is inappropriate because they are only expressing their needs in the best way they can. When babies cry and fuss they are telling us that something is wrong. They are tired, hurt, uncomfortable, hungry, wet, scared, or needing to be held.

One of the hardest times to deal with a crying infant is at night, when a wakeful baby may truly seem "bad." If you have been giving to your child all day long you may feel drained and resentful when you have to give again at night. You may grit your teeth when awakened at 3 AM and feel overwhelmed by your child. But if you can think of your baby as someone expressing needs rather than someone being "bad," you may feel more accepting.

Once you understand that your baby's crying is a kind of communication, you may find yourself responding differently to him, trying to understand why he cries or why he doesn't sleep as much as you think he should, or as you would like. And you may also feel less harassed when your baby fusses in public. It is easier to be comfortable with your child when you no longer feel pressured to have a "good" baby.

My Child Is Anxious About Strangers and Separation

A baby, until the age of 6 months or so, usually is content to be held by relatives and family friends; she may even smile and play when her parents place her in someone else's arms. But between the ages of 7 and 8 months, she will begin to resist people other than her parents and may cry and reach for her parents when someone else tries to hold her. During this stage, she may even feel anxious about her grandparents and familiar babysitters.

Such reactions, which are a normal part of a baby's development, result from her growing awareness of the world. She recognizes her parents as special and different and she views them with pleasure. Because she has good feelings about them, she wants to be with her parents and is not as comfortable or trusting with other people.

Also, at this age a baby believes that something exists only as long as she can see it. When her parents walk out of sight, she feels anxious about the separation, and cries. When she is back in her parents' arms, she feels pleasure.

This developmental stage, which usually doesn't last long, can be difficult for parents because it sometimes causes embarrassment and makes it hard to accept help with child care. A relative or friend, offering to care for the baby, may feel rejected by the child's anxious cries. Some adults may blame the parents, saying, "You've spoiled her by holding her so much!" Or they may try to persuade the baby to come, saying, "I won't hurt you. You have to get used to others."

When your baby enters this developmental stage, remember that anxiety about strangers and separation is normal. It isn't necessary to force your baby to go to other people—she will soon do that willingly. Just try to meet her needs, and have others talk to her and play with her while you hold her. You can explain to people that, while you understand their feelings of frustration and rejection, you know that your child is acting as most children her age do.

During this stage, many babies have trouble separating from their parents when a babysitter comes. Explain the situation to your babysitter and let her know that your baby may need extra holding and comforting when you're gone. If your child cries as you go, you may also find it hard to separate, even though you know your child usually settles down in 5 or 10 minutes. Have your babysitter try to distract your baby, and call home shortly after leaving if you'd like to reassure yourself that all is going well.

At times you might be tempted to leave while your baby is in another room, unaware that you are going. While this eliminates the initial rush of tears, your child may react with surprise and fear when she discovers you have left. It is always better to say a quick goodbye.

You will know that your child's fear of strangers and separation is lessening when you see her reach for someone other than you, and when you see her go happily to someone who is reaching for her. As this stage passes, your child will once again feel more comfortable and content with others.

My Child Is Attached to His Blanket and Other Objects

A child clutching a blanket—it is a familiar sight. Between the ages of 6 and 9 months, many young children become attached to a security object such as a blanket or stuffed animal. The attachment may last until the child is 5 or older. This is a natural part of development, although not all children pick out a special object, and some choose several soft items to hold on to. A child with a strong attachment may wake up clutching his blanket and hold it as his parents pick him up. He may put the blanket against his face and carry it around with him as he gets older.

To a young child, a blanket or other soft object is a source of comfort. As the child moves away from infancy and his close union with his mother, he nurtures and cares for his special object, receiving warmth and comfort in return. He may use his blanket most often during times of transition throughout the day—when he goes to sleep, wakes up, feels tired or hurt, goes for a car trip, visits the doctor, goes to a babysitter's house, etc.—and during major changes in his life or routine. These can include the birth of a sibling, the beginning of nursery school, or a parent's absence. Children who are left to cry themselves to sleep or whose dependency needs are not consistently met may become particularly dependent on an object for comfort.

The child's attachment to his special object may go through

different stages. At times he will have an intense need for his blanket and will let his parents know that he wants it, even if he can't yet tell them in words. At other times, during calm periods and as he gets older, he may have less need for the special object.

One child, who developed a strong attachment to a stuffed animal given to her when she was a few months old, took the toy everywhere she went. But when she turned 4, her attachment began to lessen. First she threw the animal out of her bed, although she quickly retrieved it. Then she began moving it, night by night, into less favorable positions on her bed. She stopped hugging and sleeping with the animal and eventually, when she no longer needed it, she put it away on a shelf.

If your child is attached to a special object, you may find it hard to trust that he will ever give it up. You may wonder if you should remove the object or wean your child away from it, but such actions are unnecessary. As time goes on, your child's desire for his object will diminish and he will give it up on his own. However, you may not see this happen until your child is 5, since many 4- and 5-year-olds keep their objects with them at night as a source of comfort. Interestingly, when parents recognize how strong and long-lasting their child's attachment is, they sometimes begin to feel protective of the object themselves.

Should I Give My Child a Pacifier?

A generation ago, pacifiers were in great disfavor. Today, although there are still critics, there are many more pediatricians, hospital nurseries, and parents offering pacifiers to babies.

A baby feels calm when her natural sucking instinct is satisfied. Some babies suck their thumbs, some nurse frequently, some suck on fingers or a blanket, and many use pacifiers. When parents first offer a pacifier to their child, they see how tranquil she becomes and how convenient the pacifier is to use. It's an easy, concrete, accessible way to soothe a crying child. Parents can offer it in the car, leave it in the crib so their child can suck as she falls asleep, or, as she gets older, leave it near her toys so she can use it whenever she wants.

There is nothing wrong with a pacifier, and a child who uses one is not harmed in any way. Yet, despite growing acceptance, there are people who believe pacifiers symbolize dependency and immaturity, especially when used by a child past infancy. A parent can easily feel under attack when told, "That thing looks awful hanging out of her mouth," or "She's much too old to use a pacifier."

Parents look to their pediatricians for advice and support on all aspects of childrearing, including matters such as pacifier use, but there are pediatricians who oppose pacifiers. One mother, who believed her child should use a pacifier, never let her child take it along on doctor visits because the pediatrician disapproved. It was easier for this mother to hide what she did rather than face ridicule or a challenge to her parenting beliefs.

Aside from dealing with outside criticism, many parents of children using pacifiers have their own doubts. When and how will the child ever give up such a comforting and satisfying object?

Children do give it up. Gradually, and in spite of the strong attachment you may now observe, your child will limit her use of the pacifier to times when she is tired or feeling stress. By age 2, she may wean herself completely from it, or at least let you know, by rejecting it at times or accepting it less often, that she's ready to stop using it.

However, if you decide to take your child's pacifier away before she shows a willingness to give it up on her own, do so gradually, over several weeks. And be prepared for the possibility that she will begin sucking her thumb, blanket or other object. Offer substitutes for the pacifier such as a glass of juice, extra holding and cuddling, gentle patting on the back, or a new source of comfort such as a stuffed animal or pillow.

My Child Sucks His Thumb

People's reactions vary when they see a child sucking his thumb. Some feel strongly that it is good for the child to fulfill his own needs this way, while others feel just as strongly that it is bad for the child. Because of the differing opinions offered on the subject, parents are sometimes unsure about what to do if their child sucks his thumb.

Babies begin sucking their thumbs for the same reasons they use pacifiers and frequent nursing or bottle drinking—to satisfy their sucking needs. The thumb is always there and so the child is always in control, which is not the case with the pacifier, breast, or bottle. And a baby who sucks his thumb may be less dependent on his parents to calm and soothe him since, with his thumb, he is able at times to comfort himself.

It is not unusual for a child to suck his thumb for years—sometimes until he is 5 or 6, or even older. During the preschool years sucking gradually decreases, and by the time the child is of school age, he is usually sucking his thumb only at night before bed or during an anxious time, such as the birth of a sibling or a move to a new house. Some children, however, may occasionally suck their thumbs during the day when they first enter elementary school.

There are pediatricians who advocate thumbsucking and even encourage new parents to help their baby get started on the habit. These doctors reason that sucking the thumb is a natural and easy way for a child to satisfy himself. Other doctors say that a child who is given the breast or bottle on demand will already have his sucking needs met and will not need or desire a thumb. Finally, there are pediatricians who are against thumb-sucking, believing it an unnecessary habit that may harm the child's teeth.

Just as doctors offer various opinions, parents, too, have different feelings about thumbsucking. Many parents are un-concerned about their child's habit, but feel bothered by the negative comments they hear from others. Friends, relatives, and even strangers will criticize a child for thumbsucking, and will try to pressure his parents to stop him. For many families, this is the only problem connected with thumbsucking—inter-ference from non-family members.

In other families, thumbsucking is looked on with ambiva-lence. Parents worry about their child's teeth, about how long he will continue his habit, about how he will finally give it up, and about whether they should try to make him stop. And there are parents who do not want their child to suck his thumb at all. These parents worry about how to stop him right away.

What are parents' choices? If parents notice this habit during their child's early months, they can try to nurse or bottle feed more frequently, which may satisfy his sucking needs. Other-wise, parents can accept thumbsucking as a natural habit, and try to make the best of it even if they don't like it, or they can try to force the child to stop. This latter course can have negative consequences for the child and is usually unsuccessful because a thumb, unlike a pacifier, can't be taken away. If the parents pull a child's thumb out of his mouth, he will cry and then most likely suck his thumb again as soon as he can. And, as the child gets older, if they paint his thumb with one of the foul-tasting commercial products sold to discourage thumbsucking, the child will feel helpless and may whine, show increased aggression, or become obstinate.

Since sucking provides comfort, the more pressure parents

put on their child to stop, the more attached and dependent on his thumb he may become. Fearing ridicule, and feeling vulnerable, the child may depend more and more on himself and his thumb for comfort. This is not an attempt to rebel or get back at his parents, although parents may see increased thumbsucking as stubbornness or "badness." The child has a strong desire to please his parents, but he also has a strong desire to suck his thumb in order to make himself feel better. One 4-year-old child who knows her parents disapprove of her thumbsucking hides under a table when she wants to suck her thumb. Parents who want their child to stop his habit should try decreasing the pressure they put on him. This, in turn, may eliminate some of his need to soothe himself with increased thumbsucking.

Another drawback to struggling over thumbsucking is the bad self-image a child can eventually develop when he senses that his parents don't like what he is doing. Parents who try to make their child feel bad about his habit ("No, no, bad boy! I don't like that!") may end up having the child feel bad about himself. Some parents can remember back to their own childhood embarrassment and pain over the issue of thumbsucking.

The best thing you can do if your child sucks his thumb is accept the situation and be patient. Try not to discourage him from thumbsucking, at least through his preschool years when his need may be strongest. Usually by 5 or 6 the child will give up sucking his thumb because his friends have stopped, because he no longer has the need, or because he is self-conscious about sucking his thumb in public.

The only time to worry about your child's thumbsucking is if, during the early elementary years, he is still sucking often during the day. Then you might want to seek professional advice about what you might do to help your child. And if you are worried about the effect of thumbsucking on your child's teeth, you should check with your pediatrician and seek a second opinion from a dentist.

Now She Needs Me,
Now She Doesn't

Parents are often puzzled when their toddler shifts from being dependent to being independent and back again. Why, for example, would the child suddenly dart away from her mother and then just as suddenly come running back to check that her mother is still there?

Such on and off behavior comes from the child's mixed feelings about her place in the world. When she first learns to walk, she develops a sense of independence and joy. She is delighted with her new-found skill and control, feeling that the world is at her command. Soon after exercising her new independence, however (sometime between 17 months and 2 years), her perceptions of her place in the world change and she feels quite small and vulnerable. It is her joy in exploration combined with her feelings of inadequacy that lead her to run off and run back.

Typical of a child at this stage is an 18-month-old girl waiting in line with her mother at the post office. The girl wiggles away from her mother and goes to look at a chain hanging across a doorway. As soon as she reaches the chain she says, "Mommy, Mommy," and runs to get picked up. After a few seconds she gets back down, runs and touches the chain, and then runs back to her mother. The girl repeats this cycle as long as she and her mother wait in line.

This developmental phase of emotional dependence-independence, which is a normal part of growth, can last until the child is 2½ to 3 years old. Different children show different degrees of dependence: some children are not comfortable exploring their surroundings on their own and may cling to their parents. Most children need more reassurance when they are out of their secure and comfortable homes.

During this stage, your child may be especially sensitive to your responses and may be easily upset when you disapprove of her behavior, just as she is pleased when you approve. Over time, as your child gains more experience, a change will occur and she will be able to play, explore, and move about without coming to you for repeated reassurance. Until then, try to accept her behavior, smile and wave when she goes off a bit on her own, and give her the emotional support she needs to feel secure about her world.

My Child Likes to Be
Where I Am

Young children want to be near their parents. While the intensity of need varies with age and personality, children, especially between the ages of 15 months and 3 years, are usually most content playing and exploring when their parents are close by.

A baby will indicate his need for closeness by reaching out to be picked up. When the child can crawl, he will follow his parents' voices and crawl to be near them. Later, as a toddler, he will often carry his toys from room to room to be with his parents. And although at 3 or 4 years old he may spend time at school, day care, or a neighbor's house, he will still prefer to be near his parents when he is home. Children, like adults, want company—especially the company of their own families.

Young children like to be with their parents much of the time, day and night. Often parents find that their child has an easier time falling asleep if they stay with him, patting his back or keeping him company. In the dark moments before sleep, an uneasy child gains comfort when his parents are near.

The child's desire to be with his parents is normal and the attention he receives from them is essential for his development. As he comes to understand that his parents are there even when he can't see them, and that every time they go away they come back, he begins to feel secure and trusting. Gradually, based on these feelings of trust, he will develop the ability and desire to separate from his parents.

Waiting for that separation to occur, however, can be frustrating for parents who would like more time to themselves. Parents don't often have a chance to be alone at home, especially when they are followed by a young child who won't let them out of his sight. And at times, a child who stays close by his parents can be an embarrassment in public or when other adults are visiting.

When your child wants to be with you, try to be understanding and accommodate him when possible, knowing that this stage of development is normal. When you need time for yourself at home, try distracting your child with an interesting puzzle, a book, or a box of toys that he hasn't played with for a while. You can invite one of your child's playmates for a visit. When your preschooler has friends over, he may play happily without having you nearby; if the children are old enough to play safely without close supervision, you can have some time to yourself.

If you are having adult guests over, try to anticipate your child's need for attention. Suggest he draw pictures for the visitors to take home. Place some interesting toys next to your seat so he can play nearby without having to involve you. Such diversions work, but it is unrealistic to expect your child to leave you entirely alone. If you exclude him, he may become demanding, silly, or whiney. But if you partially include him, focusing attention on him at least some of the time, you should be able to talk to your guests without too much interruption.

As your child reaches the early elementary years he will spend more and more time playing with friends or occupying himself in his room, and less and less time with you. One mother, whose 7-year-old son always stayed close to her when he was a pre-schooler, is surprised to find herself greatly wishing he would spend more time with her now.

"Only Mommy Do It"

Between the ages of 20 months and 3 years, some children won't let their fathers help them. When a father tries to comfort his child during the night, get her dressed, get her some juice, or even fasten her seatbelt, she resists: "No! Only Mommy do it." Young children are often strongly attached to their mothers, and during this brief developmental phase they seem to reject their fathers.

One mother no sooner got into bed after feeding her 2-month-old baby, when her 3-year-old daughter called out for water. The tired mother asked her husband to respond, but their daughter refused his help: "Not you. I want water from Mommy." To avoid a middle-of-the-night struggle, the mother got up, but the encounter was unpleasant for both parents.

This phase, although temporary, can be very frustrating. A father who wants to take an active role in caring for his child may find it hard to understand her resistance and rejection. At times he may feel like giving up and telling his wife, "You take care of her. Why should I even try?" The father's feelings may be hurt and he may show signs of resentment towards his child.

The mother's role, too, is difficult during this stage. It is hard for her to watch her husband being rejected, and hard to try and persuade her child to allow him to help. There is also more pressure on the mother to take over the work of child care.

This means the mother is always the one to get up at night, to give comfort, and to get the child ready in the morning.

Some parents try reasoning with their child ("Mommy's tired") and some try to force their child to accept the father's help. They say firmly, "If you want a drink, you will have to let Daddy get it." Sometimes such statements work, but sometimes tears and tantrums follow. It may be easier to "give in" to the child, at least during the night, and have the mother get up to get the drink. That way the family can go quickly back to sleep rather than deal with a struggle.

If the father is unable to help his child because she rejects him, he can still help his wife by taking over additional household responsibilities or caring for the couple's other children. And both parents should try not to let the father's feelings of rejection interfere with their basic relationship with their child. In the course of the child's development, the stage of "only Mommy do it" is rather short.

Why Does My Child Want Me with Him at Birthday Parties?

When a birthday invitation arrives in the mail, children are excited. They ask, "Can I go? When is it?" and talk eagerly about presents, cake, and goodie bags. But when the first excitement is over, a child may ask his parents another question: "Will you stay with me at the party?"

For some children, attending a party is difficult. Between the ages of 2 and 3½, a child may only go to a birthday party if his parents come along, and he may cling and ask them not to leave once he has arrived. This can happen even when the birthday child is a close friend and the birthday home is familiar.

Children who are shy are likely to have a harder time separating than children who are out-going and self confident. A child who is quiet in groups may prefer to observe at parties rather than to participate and may only feel comfortable doing this when his parents are with him. A child also may want his parents around because he feels temporarily overwhelmed by the excitement, the number of people at the party, the sight of strange children, or the unusual appearance of a friend's house decorated for a birthday. If the party is in a restaurant or other unfamiliar place, a child may feel even more unsure.

Some children feel insecure at parties because their friends' fathers are there; many 2- and 3-year-olds are not comfortable with other children's fathers. In some cases, children have not been around men as much as around women, and they may find fathers a bit scary because of their deep voices, big size, beards, etc. Occasionally, a child becomes afraid of a father because of the man's profession: "He's a policeman and can put you in jail," one 4-year-old told his 3-year-old brother.

Whatever the reason for a child's reluctance to attend a party alone, his parents may experience frustration because of the situation. They may wonder why their child needs to be with them when other children the same age seem willing to stay at parties by themselves: "Is my child the only one like this?" And parents may worry about their child's ability to interact with other children, or his lack of independence.

In addition, parents can become angry, especially if they have other plans for the hours of the party, or if they don't generally like to stay and participate at birthday parties. An angry parent may tell a child, "If you don't stay at the party by yourself you will have to come home right now!" Such a message can leave the child feeling unaccepted, angry, and "bad" over something that he is already having difficulty working through. And an angry parental outburst can make the parent feel bad later: "Was I too harsh?"

If parents can recall their own childhood experiences at parties, they may feel more tolerant and accepting about their child's anxieties. Most of us have mixed memories: we remember feeling good about the cake and ice cream and games, but we also remember some disappointments and feelings of shyness and embarrassment.

If your child is anxious about attending a party, you can look for ways to make him feel more comfortable. For example, see if a close friend or neighbor is invited to the same party so the two children can go together. Being with a friend may ease the pressure your child feels and may make separating from you easier.

If you take your child to the party and he wants you to remain, try staying for a few minutes to see if he begins to feel at ease. The parent giving the party can help by getting your child involved with another guest, or with a toy or game. And sometimes just showing your child the cake and goodie bags will be enough to make him feel comfortable. If he decides he can stay alone, let him know that you are leaving and tell him you will be back when the party is over.

If, however, your child wants to have you stay with him for the entire party, you may need to make spontaneous plans to do so. Tell the host that your child will feel more comfortable with you there; most parents will be understanding, especially if you offer to help out. And keep in mind that although this situation may seem difficult, your child will become more independent with time. By the age of 4 or 5, he will probably go more confidently to parties without you and enjoy participating and playing on his own.

When My Child Is Away from Me, She's Different

When parents hear how well-behaved their child is with a relative, teacher, friend, or caretaker, their response is often, "That's not how she acts when she's with me." And conversely, when parents hear that their usually energetic child seemed withdrawn while spending time away from home, they wonder, "Why does she act differently when she's away?"

A child's behavior does change, depending on whom she's with and where she is. Parents see this when they pick their child up from school, day care, or a friend's house. As soon as they arrive, their child may start acting negatively—whining, making demands, and clinging. When the parents ask if their child has acted this way all along, the usual answer is, "No, she was fine until you arrived." Parents may be partly relieved to hear their child enjoyed herself, but also partly upset by her actions.

Most often, a child's behavior changes when her parents arrive because she is more comfortable when they are around. Once she sees them, she can express the feelings she may have been keeping to herself. Perhaps the day was frustrating because she couldn't play with a favorite toy, or because a teacher put pressure on her. Or perhaps she was angry at her parents for leaving her with a babysitter. The day's frustrations all come out when her parents come to pick her up.

It is natural for a child to feel less comfortable expressing her needs and feelings when she's away from home. Adults, too, are more reserved when at work or in the company of others. Therefore, it is not surprising that a child who seems content all day will let off steam when she's with her parents.

Sometimes parents experience the opposite situation with their child. She seems happy and playful when they arrive and is reluctant to go home. The parents assume that she's had a wonderful time, but often the child has actually spent the day acting withdrawn and uninvolved. Such behavior, typical of 2-year-olds, occurs because the child is more comfortable playing and exploring when her parents are around. Therefore, she doesn't really begin to enjoy herself until it's time to leave.

If your child seems fussy after a day away from you, or starts complaining when it's time to go home, be sure to question the teacher, friend, or babysitter who has been caring for her. Ask about your child's interests and activity level, and try to get a true picture of her day. When communication is good between you and your child's caregivers, you will be better able to anticipate and understand your child's behavior.

If you know that your child's mood will change when she sees you, you can plan ahead. If she's whining, try to distract her: "When we get home, I'm going to get the play dough out." And if you know she will want to start playing when you are ready to pick her up from school or day care, plan to arrive a little early or stay a little longer. That way, your child will have time to explore comfortably and then leave in a pleasant way.

SLEEPING

When Will My Baby Sleep Through the Night?

"Does your baby sleep through the night yet?" That's a familiar question for new parents, and one they dread answering if their child is still waking up. Many people believe that a baby should be sleeping through the night by the time he is 3 months old, and if he isn't, his parents may naturally feel frustrated and worried. Losing sleep is one of the hardest adjustments new parents have to make.

Actually, it is rare for an infant consistently to sleep through the night. Some babies do sleep through when they are 3 weeks old, but many are still waking up at 10 months and others are 2 or 3 years old before they sleep all night. The frequency of waking varies from child to child and depends on many circumstances.

An infant may wake up at night because he needs to be fed, changed, or held. A slightly older child, one who has learned to roll from his front to his back, may turn himself over during the night, waking up in the process. If a baby has new teeth coming in, he may be uncomfortable and wake up to be comforted. And if a child is developmentally at the stage when he believes people exist only if he can see them, he may wake up to see his parents and be reassured. Parents often consider this last type of wakefulness to be manipulative because the child stops crying as soon as they come in his room. But the child

33

does not intend to manipulate—he just wants to see his parents and be close to them.

Basically, a child wakes up because he needs to be loved, comforted, fed, or helped. A young child does not understand that his parents prefer to meet his needs during the day and sleep during the night. He wants his parents whenever he needs them—day or night.

A wakeful baby can be difficult and frustrating for parents. If they get up at night to respond to their child, they lose sleep and suffer all the physical and emotional consequences of being tired. They also face the criticism of others who say, "The only way your baby is going to learn to sleep is if you let him cry it out." Such comments are unfortunate because parents who do get up at night with their children need support and encouragement. Many of these parents eventually become secretive about getting up because they don't want to be ridiculed by friends and relatives.

Sometimes parents of a wakeful child become resentful, envying other parents whose children sleep all night, and wondering what is wrong with their own child: "Does everyone else have an easier baby?" Parents may blame themselves for their situation, believing that they caused their child's wakefulness by being too attentive to his cries: "If only we had let him cry it out earlier, maybe we'd all be sleeping now."

There's really no need for doubt and self-blame. Parents who go to their child at night give him a sense of security and show him that they care about his needs. When a child is left to cry it out at night (which is what many child care advisors advocate) he learns only that he has no options, that his needs will not be consistently met, and that his only choice is to give up. It is important to go to a child who wakes up crying at night.

Parents of a wakeful child need to know that they are not alone. Many babies wake up during the night. One mother, who was frequently up with her child in the middle of the night, took comfort looking out at the house next door. There she saw a brightly lit window indicating that their neighbors were awake with their own infant. This mother felt relieved knowing that other people were going through the same thing she was. Once parents understand this—that they are not alone—they can alter their expectations about normal sleeping patterns and begin to feel better about their child's behavior.

If you are the parent of a wakeful child, you will want to help your child get back to sleep as quickly as possible. First, try to meet his needs by changing him, feeding him, or making him more comfortable. If he is still wakeful, try soothing him with rocking or singing. Sometimes mechanical, repetitive sounds calm a baby. On a "loop" tape you can record the hum of a hair dryer, humidifier, air conditioner, fan, even a vacuum cleaner, and play it when your baby needs to be comforted. There are also special tapes, records, and teddy bears that play the sounds of heartbeats; you might try one of these. You can also try staying with your child in his room, rubbing his back until he falls asleep. Or you might want to bring him back to bed with you so he can nurse or just calm down while you sleep. Having your child sleep with you may be less exhausting and frustrating than getting up several times to comfort and feed him.

If you are not getting enough sleep, try napping during the day or early evening, or going to bed early at night. And recognize that, exhausting as this part of child care can be, wakefulness will decrease as your child gets older. Eventually, you will get a full night's sleep again.

My Child Won't Fall
Asleep Alone

Many parents have problems getting their children to sleep at night. When it's time for bed, a child may want to be nursed, held, walked, sung to, talked to, read to, or comforted. The child would like her parents to spend time with her as she falls asleep, but her parents would rather put her quickly and peacefully to bed and then get on with their own activities.

Parents wonder why their child won't fall asleep alone when they hear, or imagine, that other people's children go to sleep easily. It's true that some children quickly fall asleep, and that others are content to lie down with a bottle, pacifier, blanket, or stuffed animal. But most young children have a genuine need for their parents to be with them at night.

Bedtime can be a lonely, frightening time for young children, who naturally feel safer and more comfortable if their parents stay with them. Even 3-, 4-, and 5-year-olds prefer not to be alone at night. One child said, "I can fall asleep better if you stay in my room," and another asked her parents, "Why do you want me to go to sleep? Don't you want to be with me?" A child finds it hard to understand her parents' need to be alone—she obviously has no such need herself.

The intensity of a child's bedtime need for her parents can be judged by the struggles that occur when her parents leave her in her room. A baby might spend a long time crying while an older child might get up or call out for water, another kiss, a trip to the bathroom, and anything else that would bring her parents close again. Elaborate bedtime rituals can take 40 minutes or longer and often leave parents angry and frustrated. It's not unusual for a parent to sing "Rock-a-Bye Baby" through clenched teeth.

But what happens if, instead of spending 40 minutes trying to get the child to fall asleep alone, parents spend 10 to 20 minutes keeping their child company—nursing her or rubbing her back or lying next to her? The child will feel content and secure and fall asleep peacefully without a bedtime struggle.

Once parents see how strong their child's need and desire for closeness is, they may choose to stay with her at bedtime. In this situation, as in many others, parents will have to lower their expectations: they will have less free time than they would like. But they will also eliminate many nighttime problems associated with a child's loneliness, fear, and insecurity, and they will end their child's day in a calm and relaxed way.

If you decide to stay with your child until she falls asleep, you may find that few people you discuss the situation with will give you support and encouragement. Many parents do stay with their children, but few talk about it because they fear criticism. In a parent discussion group, one mother blurted out that her child would not fall asleep unless she was nursed. The mother expected to hear criticism, but instead saw other mothers at the meeting nod their heads. Their children behaved the same way.

The time you spend helping your child fall asleep should be restful for both of you. You can use the time to relax, think, enjoy your child's closeness, or read. At times you will probably nap or even fall asleep for the night—a problem for some parents who would rather stay awake.

You may be afraid that if you stay with your child at bedtime she will become manipulative or unwilling ever to fall asleep alone. It's true that your child will get used to having you with her, but as she gets older her need for your company will lessen. And when you think she is ready, you can let her know that you expect her to fall asleep alone most of the time, perhaps with the help of soothing music, a night light, or other comforting device. At that point she will know that she can count on you, and that when she really needs you, you will come.

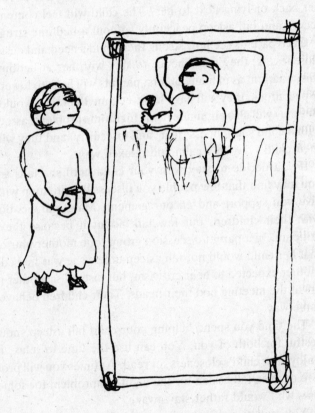

My Child Wants to Sleep in Our Bed

A young child often needs his parents during the night. As an infant he may wake up crying for them, and as a toddler he may call out for them or get out of bed to find them. Some parents meet their child's nighttime needs by going to his room and comforting him there. But other parents find it easier at times to let their child sleep in bed with them. These parents believe that they and their child sleep better when they are all together.

The thought of a child sleeping with his parents shocks some people who have been conditioned by "experts" to believe the experience is harmful. Many parents who let their child sleep with them at night are reluctant to discuss the issue because they think their situation is unique. Actually, many parents have their children sleep in bed with them at some point, and many find the experience easy, enjoyable, and beneficial.

Children end up in their parents' beds for a variety of reasons. Parents might bring a wakeful infant to bed so they can tend to him without having to get up during the night. Or they might want him near so they can be sure he's safe, and so he can feel emotionally secure. Parents of a toddler may find their child climbing into bed with them on his own during the night. While some toddlers sleep easily in their rooms, others are too frightened or lonely to stay by themselves and try desperately to sleep with their parents. A child who is determined to be with his parents may climb out of his crib or bed and go to their room. One child told his parents, "I think of scary things in my bed, but when I get into your bed they go away." If a child's parents won't let him into their bed, he might try to sleep on the floor next to their bed or sleep in the hallway outside their bedroom door.

Parents who do choose to let their child sleep with them may still express concerns about the issue. They wonder if they are being too responsive to their infant or toddler, or if he will become too dependent on them. It is true that the child may develop a habit of sleeping in his parents' bed, but he will not be harmed by this. Rather, he will benefit from the reassurance and sense of security he receives from such closeness.

When parents start letting their child sleep with them, they may wonder if they will ever again have a bed to themselves. Parents of a 9-month-old can feel overwhelmed by the thought that their child may be in bed with them for a few years, although actually, children's sleeping patterns and needs are hard to predict and parents' expectations change as children develop. The amount of time a child will spend in his parents' bed varies between families and within families over time. Some parents have their infant with them for the first 6 months to a year. Others let their child fall asleep in their bed and then move him to his own room each night; he may spend the whole night there or wake up and come back to his parents' room. Some children spend part of every night with their parents while others come to their parents' bed only occasionally.

Ultimately, the parents' goal is to have their child sleep on his own, and as the child becomes less dependent on their reassurance (usually by the time he is 4 or 5 years old) he will be ready to spend nights in his own bed. At that point parents can help their child get used to sleeping in his room by offering a night light, music, or an occasional back rub.

Parents wonder how their sexual relations will be affected by the presence of a child in bed. Since sexual relations should always be private from children, parents should not become intimate when their child is in bed with them. They can either be together in another room in the house, or carry their sleeping child back to his own room. To assure privacy, parents should close the bedroom door when they are having sexual relations. And if the child does surprise them during an intimate moment, they should try not to overreact to the intrusion. The chances are good that the sleepy child has not observed his parents very closely. Although parents might feel that the child who sleeps with them interferes with sexual spontaneity, they should remember that a child who wakes up crying in his own room also interrupts his parents' intimacy.

Aside from effects on sexual relations, there is another aspect to having a child in bed that parents are sometimes concerned about—the quality of sleep. While many parents are happy to avoid getting up with their children at night, other parents find that having a child in bed is not very restful. An infant makes many sounds as he sleeps, and a toddler may toss and turn, waking his parents. Some pediatricians recommend that parents buy themselves a queen or king size bed so they can accommodate their child. Another possibility is for parents to place a mattress or crib in their room so the child can sleep nearby.

Most parents who let their child sleep in bed with them are pleased with the results. Parents who are away from their child all day enjoy the chance to be close to him at night, to give a middle-of-the-night hug and say, "I love you," and to wake up next to him in the morning. Parents often report that their child doesn't have nightmares and has fewer problems falling asleep when he is in bed with them. And families tend to get more sleep when parents don't have to wake up and go to a child in another room.

If you are concerned about having your child in your bed,

remember that there are different ways to meet your child's needs. If you are comfortable going to your child's room, that is a good choice for you. And if you prefer bringing your child back to your own room, that also is fine. Whichever way you choose to respond, the important thing is to give your child the security that comes with attention and care.

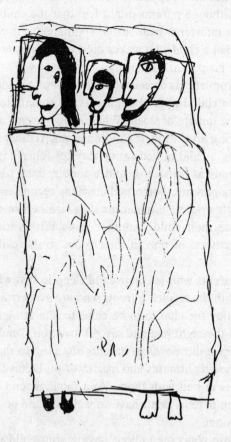

I Want My Child to Play in Her Crib When She Wakes Up

Parents always value the times when their child wakes up and plays contentedly in her crib. An infant may be entertained by looking at or randomly batting a mobile, and a baby who can sit up may be happy with toys left for her. The cheerful sounds of a child playing in her crib are delightful to parents—and so are the extra bits of free time that come when the child entertains herself.

The length of time a child will spend playing alone varies, depending on her age and needs. Some children will play happily as long as they hear their parents nearby, while others will stop playing and want to be picked up as soon as they hear their parents. Many babies won't play at all and want to be taken out of the crib as soon as they are awake. It is not unusual for babies to go through different phases: a child who has been happy to play in her crib may suddenly stop wanting to spend time there. And often, a child who shows anxiety about being separated from her parents during the day will not want to play alone in her crib.

If your child doesn't play when she wakes up, you probably feel frustrated, especially if she is an early riser. In order to get a little more sleep, you might try bringing your child back to bed with you when she first wakes up. Even if she doesn't fall asleep again, she may lie quietly with you for a while. You can also put some toys on your bed or on the floor nearby and encourage your child to play quietly while you rest.

If your child does play in her crib, be sure the toys you leave for her are safe and appropriate. And since a child does a lot of moving and turning while she sleeps, be sure the objects in her crib will not harm her or wake her up if she bumps them. You might also want to switch toys in the crib every few weeks so your child will have some new things to play with. And occasionally try putting your child in her crib to play after a bath or meal—you might have a little extra time to yourself if she is content to stay there for a while.

What About Nap Time?

Since parents spend a lot of time giving to their child and putting off their own needs, they look forward to the free time they have when their child naps. While parents are adjusting to their newborn, they often use free time to catch up on sleep. But gradually they feel the need to be "productive" during their child's nap time and may plan to do something during that period every day.

Each child has his own pattern of napping which changes as he grows. During the first months of infancy, a child may spend most of the day sleeping and then, for the next six months to a year, nap several hours at a time in the morning and again in the afternoon. Over the next year, he will most likely drop one of these naps and then gradually give up napping altogether. Of course, there are many children who stop napping at 1½ years old, and others who never take predictable naps, even in infancy. Some parents are flexible about naps and let their children follow their own natural sleep patterns, while other parents are advocates of strict scheduling.

A child's napping pattern may depend on the amount of sleep he gets at night. A child who sleeps 9 or 10 hours at night will probably need an afternoon nap, while a child who sleeps 12 hours may not need to sleep again during the day. By the time a child is 2 or 2½ years old, his napping might interfere with his nighttime sleeping so that if he naps for several hours he may be filled with energy at 10 or 11 PM. This is fine if his parents' schedules permit late morning sleeping, or if they like to spend the evening hours with him. But if they want him to go to bed earlier, they might have to try and keep him from napping or at least from napping so long. Some parents are especially reluctant to let their child nap in the car, since a few minutes of sleeping there can take the place of a much longer nap at home.

Keeping a child from napping, however, can sometimes cause problems. Some children are very irritable when they don't sleep during the day, and their parents might decide that eliminating the nap is not worth the struggle. The child might go to bed earlier if he doesn't nap, but if he is unhappy all afternoon and evening, the family has not gained much. Similarly, many children are tired and irritable if their nap is cut short, although some children are able to wake up after a short nap feeling rested and ready to play.

Children in day care often nap as they would at home. Infants sleep when they need to, and older children, who are usually up early in the mornings, generally nap for a couple of hours. These naps keep children from being sleepy during the early evening hours and allow parents extra time with their children at night.

Many young children only fall asleep for their nap when nursed or given a bottle. Some children who do not want to separate from their parents or their play may need to be rocked or patted to sleep.

If your child does not nap regularly, you may naturally feel frustrated at the lack of time for yourself. But you shouldn't try to force your child to nap, since there will be negative consequences. Your child may spend long periods crying and you will probably become angry at him and angry at yourself for forcing the issue. Instead, look for alternatives to napping. You can hire a babysitter to play with your child several afternoons a week so you can have time alone, or you can try waking your child up earlier in the morning so he will go to sleep earlier at night. As your child reaches preschool age you might try having him stay in his room for a short quiet period of reading and playing. And if none of these possibilities works out, you will still have some evening hours to yourself after your child goes to sleep.

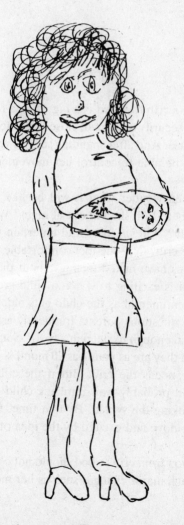

When Should My Child
Sleep in a Bed?

Moving from a crib to a bed is a big change for a toddler. She will leave the security of a small, closed-in space for the freedom of a larger space. And after spending several years in a confining crib, she will be able to control her movements in and out of bed.

Parents often wonder what it will be like when their child has her own bed. Will she fall out at night? Will she get out of bed frequently? Will she play and entertain herself in bed as she did in the crib? Will she feel comfortable and secure? Parents sometimes have mixed feelings about the transition from crib to bed: it is exciting to watch a child grow, but it is also easy to feel sentimental as the child gets older.

One of the questions parents frequently ask is, "When will my child be old enough to sleep in a bed?" Some children move to a bed when they are as young as 20 months—usually because a new sibling needs the crib. But if the crib is not needed, parents should probably wait until the child is 2½ or 3 years old before making the switch. By that time, the child may be ready for the move and excited by the idea of having her own bed.

The transition from crib to bed should not come when a child is going through major changes such as her mother's return to work or the beginning of nursery school. At these times the child will probably need the security of her familiar crib. If the change to a bed is planned in anticipation of a new baby, the parents should not wait until the baby is born to make the switch but rather give their child at least three or four months to get used to sleeping in a bed.

Before you move your child out of the crib, prepare her for the change. If you are buying a new bed or sheets, you might want to take her shopping with you. Spend some time talking to her about her move from the crib, but be careful about telling her that she's getting a bed because she's "big now." Toddlers feel a desire and pressure to be older and sometimes the suggestion that they should act "big" adds stress to a situation. Your child may feel you want her to do something she's not yet ready for.

Once you have the bed, try putting it right next to your child's crib so she can make a gradual switch from one to the other. She can begin by taking naps in the bed, then slowly start spending nights there. If your child was used to having toys in her crib, put some on her bed. After a few weeks, when she no longer needs her crib, take it down, letting her help. Or, if you are going to use the crib for a new baby, let your child help move it to the other room.

If you are concerned about your child's safety in a bed, you can buy a safety bar that will keep her from falling out. You can also put the boxspring and mattress on the floor rather than on a frame so your child can climb in and out of bed easily without getting hurt, and can even jump safely.

During the time of transition, notice how your child feels about the change. If she is having a difficult time giving up her crib, slow down. Even if you planned to use the crib for a new baby, you can postpone the change by putting the newborn in a cradle or portable crib for several months. And when you do give the crib to the baby, don't be surprised if your older child still shows an interest in playing or sleeping in it. Children occasionally like to pretend they are babies and go back to familiar objects and places. As long as your child doesn't feel pressure to give up her crib before she's ready, her transition to a bed should be smooth.

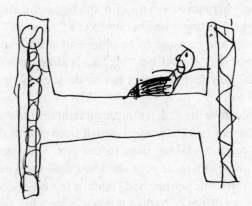

When Will My Child Stop Needing Diapers at Night?

Between the ages of 2½ and 3½, most children learn to use the toilet during the day. However, learning to stay dry at night sometimes takes another 6 months, and many children occasionally wet at night until they are 4 or 5 years old. Nighttime control generally comes later than day control because a child must go for many hours without using a toilet, and because a sleeping child can't consciously decide to go to the bathroom.

A child will stay dry at night when he is ready. He may tell his parents that he wants to stop wearing diapers, or his parents may decide that he's ready because he has been consistently dry for many days. Sometimes a child who is dry at night will find it hard to give his diapers up, but if his parents let him know that diapers are available at night if he needs them, the child will probably switch to pants without a problem. Parents should not be alarmed if their child asks to go back to wearing a nighttime diaper. Such a request is usually just a temporary desire to re-experience something familiar.

Some parents choose to help their child stay dry at night by waking him up to use the bathroom, especially if he has had a lot to drink before bed. Other parents encourage their child to be a "big boy," although such urging misses the point. A child will be dry when he is mature enough and when his body is ready. Pressuring him to act older will not help, and neither will shaming him or trying to make him feel guilty about wetting.

Even if a child has been dry for weeks or months, accidents are inevitable. If your child wets his bed, keep in mind that he is not doing it to frustrate or harass you. Either he is not quite ready to give up diapers or, if the accidents are occasional, he is sleeping too deeply to get himself to the bathroom. It is also possible that your child is reacting to the temporary stress of a move, a new baby in the family, the start of school, etc.

Whether your child has been having accidents, or has not yet been dry enough to give up diapers, you probably feel impatient and frustrated. You may feel that he has been in diapers long enough, or that you don't want to wash and change sheets frequently. These feelings are understandable, but once you realize that he will be dry as soon as he is able, you can adjust your expectations and relax. If, by the time your child is 4 or 5, he is still consistently wetting the bed, you may want to talk to your pediatrician about the situation.

EATING

Scheduled or Demand Feeding?

Infants do not have the ability to control or postpone their needs. If they are hungry or need to be comforted, they desire immediate gratification. When parents respond to their infant's cries, providing food and comfort, the baby begins to trust her world and to feel some small ability to affect what happens to her. If her cries for food are ignored, she has no way to satisfy herself.

Feeding an infant on demand, which means offering the bottle or breast whenever the baby begins to fuss, is one way parents can meet their child's needs. Demand-fed babies and their parents are usually calmer and more content then families with babies fed on a schedule. This is because an infant fed on demand does less crying for food and comfort, and her parents spend less time distracting her since she doesn't have to be held off until a scheduled feeding. A demand-fed baby may also be easier to put to sleep since she can be soothed with nursing or a bottle when she seems tired. There is no danger of overfeeding a demand-fed child; an infant will not drink more than she wants or needs.

Parents who do not choose to feed their baby on demand, but rather on a schedule, often find themselves trying to comfort or put off their crying child. The baby might want to be fed, but the parents feel that it is too soon, that the baby should wait three or four hours because she has "just fed." While it is true that some babies can easily wait four hours between feedings, it is equally true that some babies need feeding every half hour and that most have needs that fall somewhere between these extremes.

If a baby fed on a schedule is hungry before feeding time, her parents will have to play with her, hold her, and try to soothe her. And if they are not able to calm her down, they may be likely to leave her fussing or crying for long periods of time. Since it is often hard for parents to listen to their child cry, this can be a difficult situation, and one that probably takes as much time and energy as the extra feedings given to a demand-fed child.

New parents often decide to feed their child on a schedule because of advice from friends, relatives, and the infant's pediatrician. In the face of such advice, parents find it difficult to trust their instincts and begin demand feeding. Some parents also worry that demand feeding means giving in to their child and letting her have too much control. Yet an infant, because she is helpless, needs to feel she has some control, some ability to make other people respond. When her needs are met, she learns to trust that her parents will take care of her.

The decision to demand-feed or feed on a schedule is often influenced by the way the child is fed—by breast or bottle. Although either method can be adapted to scheduled or demand feeding, it is more likely that a breast-fed baby will be demand-fed, if only because of the ease of feeding. A mother can easily offer her breast at any time, while the parents of a bottle-fed infant must first prepare and warm bottles and formula.

A bottle-fed infant is more likely to be fed on a schedule because her parents can easily see how much milk she is drinking, and thus can decide when they think she has had enough. Parents of a breast-fed baby, on the other hand, do not know how much their child is drinking. When she cries soon after nursing, her mother is likely to offer the breast again because the child might not have had enough milk at the last feeding.

You can be successful breast feeding or bottle feeding your child, but using either method you will meet your child's needs best if you feed her on demand. If you feel you must follow a schedule, be flexible enough to offer the breast or bottle when your child truly seems to need it. When comforting doesn't work between scheduled feedings, your child's cries probably mean she is hungry or so tired she needs to soothe herself to sleep with the bottle or breast. At such times you should ignore the clock, follow your instincts, and meet your child's needs.

When Should I Wean?

It is hard for parents to follow their young child's lead, especially when it comes to weaning. A child will nurse or use a bottle only as long as he needs to, but most parents don't trust that their child will stop on his own. Instead, parents try to hurry their child by taking away the bottle, breast, or pacifier before the child is ready.

There is a lot of pressure on parents to wean their child. The pressure can be strong when the child reaches 1 year old, and increases as the child grows. Friends and relatives ask, "What's he doing with a bottle? Can't he drink from a cup yet?" The pediatrician may say, "He doesn't need to nurse or use a bottle anymore." One mother reluctantly weaned her 21-month-old son after such a statement from his doctor, although the child still enjoyed the bottle. Even passersby may comment, "He's too big for a bottle." Negative remarks are directed not just at the child, but at the parents. "What's wrong with you? Why are you still nursing?" "Why don't you take his bottle away?"

Parents feel especially self-conscious when judged by other parents. If the parents of a 2½-year-old believe theirs is the only child on the playground who still drinks from a bottle, they will wonder how it looks to other people and what other parents are thinking. They will doubt their own judgment and wonder what they've done wrong or what's wrong with their child: "Do I baby him too much? Do we give in to him?" These parents would feel better if they knew that many children are just not ready to be weaned at an early age. Parents can avoid feeling embarrassed in public by telling their young child that he will have to wait until the family is alone before he can nurse or have his bottle.

If the bottle, breast, or pacifier is taken away from a child too soon, he will probably look for other ways to satisfy his sucking needs. He might become irritable or start sucking his blanket. One mother, who threw out her 15-month-old's bottles on the advice of her pediatrician, said, "My son seems OK but he started sucking his thumb." Some breast-fed babies who are weaned at 12 to 18 months may not yet be ready to give up sucking. If these children are only offered a training cup and not a bottle, they may suck the top of the cup.

Many children who drink frequently and successfully from a cup still nurse or use a bottle. Between the ages of 2 and 3, a child may want to suck when he is tired, feeling stress from a fall or hurt feelings, spending time with a sitter, or just relaxing with a favorite blanket or stuffed animal. He may also want a bottle whenever he sees another child with one. And during times of transition, such as a move or the arrival of a new baby, a child's sucking needs may increase.

If a child is allowed to nurse, drink from a bottle, or use his pacifier when he wants, he will eventually wean himself. Gradually, his needs will decrease until he no longer asks to nurse or drink from his bottle. This often happens by the time the child is 2 to 3, although many older children will relax before sleep with a bottle.

If parents feel they must hurry the weaning process, they should do so carefully. They should be sure that weaning will not interfere with another stage of development such as learning to use the toilet, beginning nursery school, or adjusting to a new sibling. The process should be stretched over several weeks so the child is not forced abruptly to give up something important. To ease the transition from bottle or breast to cup, the child can be offered a training cup that is easy and comfortable to use.

As your child gives up the bottle or breast, you may have ambivalent feelings. If you nursed, you may feel good about "having your body to yourself" again; or you may be glad to stop fussing with bottles. But you may also feel sad to give up the warm, close feeling you had as you held your child and offered him milk, or watched him lie contentedly with his bottle. You may also miss the free time you had when he drank quietly by himself. Whatever your feelings—impatience or reluctance—in time your child will be weaned. If you can wait until he is ready to wean himself, the process will be a simple and natural one.

My Child Puts Everything
in Her Mouth

During infancy, a child's mouth is her main source of pleasure and satisfaction. She enjoys sucking at the breast or bottle, drinking warm milk, and sucking on her fingers. Starting at about 6 months, the child also gets oral enjoyment and relief from teething by sucking and biting on objects around her.

Babies don't just put things in their mouths for pleasure or comfort, though—they also use their mouths for exploration. They learn about objects by tasting them, feeling their texture, and experimenting with them. Until a child is about 2 years old, many things that she plays with will eventually go into her mouth. She will pick up things from the floor, chew on her stroller safety strap, and even try to put her parents' keys in her mouth.

Because a child can't tell what is safe or unsafe to put in her mouth, parents have to be very watchful. If your child is at this oral stage, you must pick up pieces of fuzz, crumbs, and small toys so your child will not accidentally choke on them. You also have to be sure that the objects she puts in her mouth are clean.

This developmental phase may seem long and tiresome to you, but if you start pulling safe objects out of your child's mouth, or telling her that "only food should go in your mouth," you will be depriving her of pleasure and a chance to explore. Try instead to realize and accept the fact that your child has to put objects in her mouth because that is a major way she learns about her environment.

My Child Drops Food from the High Chair

Young children, especially between the ages of 10 and 18 months, tend to make a mess when they eat. As they sit in their high chairs they mash food, spread it around, and drop it on the floor—sometimes pea by pea, occasionally a bowlful at a time.

Parents wonder why their child acts this way. Is he doing it to bother them? To defy or manipulate them? Usually not. A child might throw his food down because he is finished eating and doesn't want any more, or because he doesn't like the food he's been given. He might also just be tired and ready to get down from the high chair. Often, a child makes a mess because he's playing with his food, experimenting with the textures and spreading the food around to see what happens. A young child is interested in his meal not just for its taste but for its color and feel, and he doesn't mind getting messy in his explorations.

When a child methodically drops bits of food onto the floor, he may be testing his own power over objects and his ability to make things happen. Children repeat this process because they seem to have a strong inner need to perform the same actions over and over. As a child drops his food, he feels delighted that he can control each piece, deciding where it will land and watching it fall. Feeling in control means a lot to a child because often he has no real control over important aspects of his life. He is particularly concerned at this age about separating from his parents and about his inability to keep them with him. Even so small an activity as dropping food, an activity that the child can control, may help him work out his feelings about separation.

This phase, in which the child likes to drop things (toys as well as food), can be irritating for parents. If your child is at this developmental stage, you probably find that he won't listen when you tell him to stop. This happens because your young, egocentric child cannot consider your wishes and his at the same time. He ends up considering just his own desires and drops food even when you tell him not to. If you can view this impersonally, without thinking that your child is trying to provoke you, you will probably have an easier time dealing with him.

And still there is the practical problem of cleaning up all the dropped food. You can spread newspaper or a piece of vinyl under your child's high chair so you don't have to spend time wiping the floor. And you can try putting less food on your child's tray. That way he will still have a little to experiment with while you will have less to clean.

When Should My Child
Use a Spoon and Fork?

Soon after a child begins sitting in a high chair she will probably want to try feeding herself. At first she will use her hands to pick up food, getting some in her hair, on her clothes, and on the floor. Eventually, she will become a bit neater and start eating with utensils, although she will still use her hands often.

Some parents are so bothered by messy eating that they try to stop their child from feeding herself. They think that meals will be faster and more efficient if they do the feeding, and they are probably right. Yet there are other considerations. A child can become so frustrated when she isn't allowed to touch her food or feed herself that she might push away what her parents offer and even refuse to eat. All children at some point have a desire to feed themselves, and they are usually more cooperative at the table when their parents let them try.

When your child is ready to start feeding herself, you can minimize messiness by putting only a small amount of food on the tray (although some tolerant parents let their child plunge into a whole bowlful). When your child is 10 to 14 months old, you may see signs that she is ready to try a utensil: she might reach for the spoon you are using or imitate your actions as you eat your meals or feed her.

Her first utensil should be a spoon, since it is safer to use than a fork. You can continue to feed her with your spoon while letting her dip her own spoon into the bowls of food. By the time she is 18 months old she may be ready to use a child-sized fork, as long as you watch to see she doesn't harm herself with it.

Don't be concerned about the way your child holds her utensils; if she seems comfortable and is able to get some food into her mouth, there's no need to worry. If your child seems uncomfortable, you can show her how to hold a spoon or fork correctly, but don't get into a struggle if she refuses to follow your example. Eventually she will learn by imitating you.

If your child doesn't want to use a utensil even though she is old enough, and prefers eating with her hands, try to accept the situation. She may be more successful eating with her hands, or may just prefer to touch her food directly. Since eating should be a relaxed and enjoyable experience, it is not wise to try forcing your child to use a spoon and fork. Just have utensils available so your child can try them out when she is ready. By the time she is 2½ to 3 years old she will be using utensils much of the time.

Should My Child At Least Taste Foods?

Parents want mealtime to be pleasant, enjoyable, and healthy, and they also want their children to eat a variety of foods. But often the ways in which parents try to accomplish these goals are self-defeating.

Parents may put new food in front of a child and say, "Just taste it." They hope, of course, that their child will enjoy the food and therefore ask for more. They also hope that after trying one taste, he will get used to experimenting with new foods. However, what often happens is that the child refuses the taste and a power struggle develops.

Parents sometimes try threats or various types of persuasion: "You won't get dessert unless you taste this." Using dessert as an incentive focuses too much attention on sweets and often causes a child to expect dessert as a reward. Parents also say, "But it's good for you," "It will make you big and strong," and "Some poor children don't have any food to eat." But children tend to ignore such statements, which are based in part on falsehoods. There is no instant strength from food and eating a meal won't help another child who has to go without.

Although parents may succeed in having their child taste something new, there can certainly be negative consequences. First, the child seldom, if ever, asks for more of the originally rejected food. And if the family is eating in public, the child's refusal to eat more than one bite can lead to embarrassment.

One young child, forced to taste apple pie at a friend's party, declared loudly, "I hate this dessert!" Once a child decides he doesn't want what is offered, he will seldom reverse his decision. Another negative effect of forcing children to taste food is the risk of establishing a life-long pattern of aversion. Many adults continue to avoid food they remember being forced to eat when they were children.

Basically, struggles over food are not so much about eating as they are about power: parents try to make children taste something while children try to resist their parents' pressure. Children feel powerless when they are not able to say "I don't want it." And when they do try a bite of something they don't want, they eat only because they feel they have no choice, or they want to please their parents, or they want dessert.

When a child resists food, he is usually not being stubborn. Often he decides that he likes or doesn't like something based on its looks and consistency, not on its taste. Therefore, he may know at first sight that he doesn't want to try something new. Occasionally a child may refuse to taste food because he is afraid that once he tries a bite, he will have to keep on trying more and more new foods.

Yet despite all the negative effects and emotions involved in forcing a taste, parents get into mealtime struggles for a positive reason: they want their children willingly to eat a variety of nutritious foods. And there are ways to accomplish this without resorting to arguments. You can talk to your pediatrician or a nutritionist about alternatives for a healthy diet. And there are books available with advice and recipes for preparing meals with a variety of tastes. Try providing healthy snacks that children generally enjoy, such as homemade frozen juice bars, carrots, raisins, sunflower seeds, fresh fruit, etc., and model for your child the kind of healthy eating habits you want him to adopt.

And at mealtime, provide a variety of healthful food and leave your child free to choose what he wants to eat. You will find that when there is no coercion or arguing, meals are more relaxed and children are more willing to try new foods. As your child gets older, his tastes will change, and he will eat different types and amounts of food. For pleasant and healthy eating, the best thing to do is offer a variety of good food without putting on the pressure.

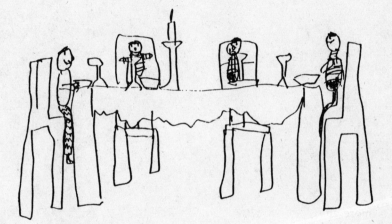

INDEPENDENCE

I Want My Child to Spend Time in a Playpen

In theory, a playpen is an excellent piece of equipment. It provides a secure place for a baby to play and it frees parents from having to closely supervise their child. The problem is that most babies spend less time in playpens than their parents would like, and many children won't stay in a playpen at all.

When parents buy a playpen, they usually think their child will play contentedly in it for long periods. They look forward to putting the playpen outside on nice days and to taking it to the beach where they will shade their child with an umbrella and let her play. When they discover their child doesn't want to spend time in the playpen, they often feel frustrated and angry, wondering why she isn't happy to stay there with all her toys.

Most children aren't content for long in a confined area. They want to explore their surroundings and move around and they want to be with their parents. Although babies' temperaments and activity levels vary, all young children have strong needs that are not met in a playpen. Some babies may play quietly there for 20 minutes, others for only a few minutes. Then they want to get out and explore or be held. One mother of a 9-month-old was determined to have her child spend a certain amount of time in the playpen each day, but the child was unhappy there and became fussy and irritable. After several weeks, the mother stopped using the playpen and found that her child was happier and more pleasant. So often children's needs don't match parents' needs.

If you want to encourage your child to spend some time in her playpen, try placing it near you so she can watch you and you can talk or play peek-a-boo with her. Give her a play object such as a toy telephone, pot, or bowl that is similar to an object you are using. Then she can occupy herself imitating you. You can also try changing the toys in the playpen frequently so your child will have something different to play with. But be careful not to clutter the playpen with too many toys.

If you see that your child is becoming frustrated, pick her up and let her explore outside the playpen. A playpen should not be the only place where your child is allowed to play. She should have a safe, childproofed space where she can move around freely. Take some of the playpen toys out and put them in the room where you are so your child can play near you. And if your child wants to be held, try using a baby carrier so you can hold her close and still accomplish something for yourself.

The playpen has its use as a safe place to put your child for short periods, but your child will never want to spend as much time there as you would like. As long as your expectations are realistic, you will probably not feel too frustrated when your child lets you know she wants to get out.

My Child Won't Hold Still During Diaper Changes

A father walked out of his son's bedroom shaking his head: "I don't believe it. He only weighs 20 pounds and I still can't get him to hold still for a diaper change." Getting a baby diapered and dressed requires a surprising amount of skill and patience, even though the job is a short one. Young children, who are usually in constant motion, squirm and resist being held down. They are excited about their world, their interests change constantly, and they want to move and explore. Because they have a hard time putting off any of their urges, even for a moment, they do not like to lie still.

Distraction can sometimes make your diapering job a little easier. Try putting some toys or interesting playthings nearby and keep handing them to your child. This might occupy him during a quick change. You can also try singing to your child or making interesting noises but most of the time you will have to restrain him a bit until you get him changed and dressed. You will naturally feel frustrated as your child resists and struggles, but just remember that your young child has a strong drive to explore and assert himself and that is why he won't hold still.

How Should I Handle Crawling?

In the middle of the first year, most babies begin crawling. This is an important stage in development, and parents watch with delight as their child becomes mobile. Although some babies start crawling before they are 6 months old, most begin between 6 and 9 months, and some never crawl, going from sitting to walking without the middle step. Because children develop at their own pace, each child will begin to crawl when she is ready. But if a child has not begun by the time she is 9 months old, her parents may want to talk to a pediatrician about her motor development.

Some parents wonder if they can motivate their baby to crawl by putting attractive toys just out of her reach. Rather than help, this may only frustrate her if she is not able to start moving. There is really no need to encourage crawling because children have an innate desire to get to many different objects and explore their surroundings. As soon as the child is developmentally ready and able to extend herself, she will start crawling.

When your child first begins to move, you may see her "belly crawl" across the floor. She will move backwards or forwards, pulling with alternating arms while her belly stays flat on the floor. Later, she will get up on all fours, rocking a little. Eventually she will move slowly on all fours, mastering the movement until she becomes a proficient crawler.

At that point (if not earlier), since your child will be able to reach many potentially dangerous objects, you will have to babyproof your house, an often time-consuming and frustrating task. You should put plants, small toys, and fragile items out of reach, but you should not stifle your child's natural curiosity about the objects she sees. As long as harmful items are out of the way, let her crawl to the curtains, touch the table leg, or reach for a toy. That is how she learns about her world. Of course, during this stage you will need to keep your floors clear of fuzz, small objects, and crumbs that could end up in your child's mouth.

You will naturally be concerned about stairs once your child is mobile. The best way to be sure your child is safe is to use gates at the top and bottom of the stairway. If you have carpeting on the steps and bottom landing, you may want to attach your gate a few steps up so your child can crawl up and down the short distance safely. However, if your landing is not carpeted, you will want to attach the gate to the bottom step to minimize harmful falls. Your child will quickly learn to climb the stairs and will enjoy going up, but most children don't learn to come down steps safely until they are at least 1 year old. That is why it is so important to close the top gate each time you pass through. Once you have made your child's environment safe, you can relax and let her enjoy crawling.

When Will My Child Start Walking?

A child will begin to walk as soon as he is developmentally ready. For some children that means at 9 months; for others, 18 months. The age at which a healthy child walks has no effect on or connection with his intelligence, yet parents often feel pressure if their child is a late walker. Friends and relatives may ask, "Are you sure he's all right? Why isn't he walking yet?" or say, "My daughter was walking when she was 10 months old and your child's already 17 months," or "Maybe your son needs to be around other children so he can learn by watching them." Such comments cause parents needless anxiety because there is nothing wrong with a developmentally healthy child who doesn't walk until he's 18 months old.

There is no need to try and teach a child to walk. Although it might be fun for parents to hold their child's hands and let him walk along, such an exercise will not help him walk alone any faster. Parents should try to be patient and wait until their child is ready for this stage of development.

A child will prepare for independent walking by first learning to pull himself up to a standing position while holding onto furniture. Once he has mastered this skill (which might take days, weeks, or even months) he will begin to take steps while holding onto furniture or onto his parent's hand. Eventually, he will let go and take some steps alone. A child who starts walking is usually so delighted with himself that he hardly notices his frequent falls.

As the child begins to stand and walk, his perspective will change. Before, he looked at everything from ground level, but once he's upright, he will see more. People, objects, and even his own body will look different. He will be able to reach more things and to roam farther and faster, and that means his parents will have to continue childproofing his environment.

You will find that one of the most delightful aspects of this developmental stage is your child's ability to go for walks with you. As soon as he's steady on his feet, take him for a leisurely stroll outside. Walk at his pace, sometimes letting him choose the direction, and see how many wonderful discoveries he makes. He will want to stop and examine pebbles, grass, worms, and flowers, and if you bring a collecting bag along, he can take some treasures home.

The more your child walks, the less he will want to use his stroller, which can cause problems when you are in a hurry or when you are going far. If you are in a crowded shopping center and want to encourage your child to stay in his stroller, try distracting him with food or a toy. If this doesn't work, try to find an uncrowded spot where he can walk for a little while without bumping into people. Often, your child will want to push the stroller himself, and in a crowd this can cause quite a fuss. If you let him push for a little while, he may be more agreeable when you place him back in his stroller. Although his slowness and desire to practice his new skill may temporarily frustrate you, you will enjoy his excitement and independence. And you may be surprised to see that once he masters walking, he will be just as likely to run as to walk.

How Different Is the View from My Child's Level?

Toddlers scramble out of their strollers, climb on anything handy, and insist on being picked up because they want to see better and reach farther. When a child stands on the floor, he can't look out of most windows. Beds and toilets seem very high and big, and doorknobs and light switches are too high up to reach.

In public places, almost nothing is placed at a child's eye level. One mother walked into a health clinic and introduced her 3-year-old son to the receptionist, who was sitting behind a high counter. The boy could not see anyone to say hello to and just stared at the wall in front of him until the woman peeked over to look at him.

When a child goes to a public bathroom, the toilets, sinks, towels, and dryers are all out of reach. Most water fountains are too high for a child to use, and most of the interesting features of stores and restaurants—cash registers, cafeteria counters, bakery bins, etc.—are out of sight. When a child has to sit in a stroller, his view is even more limited.

To see what your child sees, get down to his level and look around. You won't see your own kitchen sink or the tops of your tables. In a store, you won't be able to look at what people are doing behind counters or see most of the interesting merchandise. And you will understand why nursery schools and day care centers are so appealing to young children: everything is at eye level, and all the tables, chairs, and shelves are easy for children to reach.

Once you see how unsatisfying your child's view can be, you will understand why he wants to climb and be carried. Pick him up often so he can see what is happening around him, let him sit on store counters (while you carefully supervise), and provide safe stools or pillows at home so he can climb a little and see more of his world.

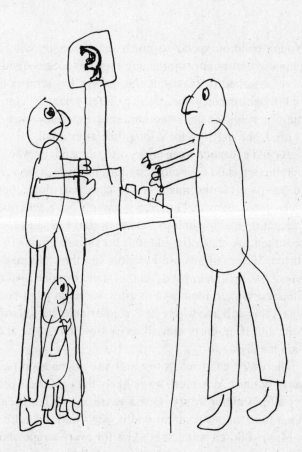

What About Falls
and Accidents?

Young children spend so much time running, climbing, and jumping that minor injuries are inevitable. Sometimes a child is so absorbed in play that she ignores her scrapes and goes right back to her game, perhaps after yelling, "You bumped me, you stupid chair." At other times, especially when the child is tired, she may cry for a long time after a fall.

A child's reaction to an injury often depends on who is around her. Since a child feels most comfortable expressing her feelings to her parents, she might cry or complain more about a fall when they are with her. Many parents have seen their child fall, get up looking unhurt, and then start crying as soon as she sees them. A child cries like this because she wants to be comforted. If her parents are not close by, the child may comfort herself or seek help from another child or adult. Adults react the same way to their own injuries: when an adult bumps into something at home where he is comfortable, he will express his pain, but if he hurts himself away from home, he is likely to hide his discomfort.

The way a child reacts to a fall also depends on her age. A very young child is much more likely than a 4- or 5-year-old to cry after a minor injury. One 5-year-old told her friend, "Just don't think about your cut and it won't hurt anymore."

Many children want Band-Aids for every scrape and bruise. Band-Aids seem magical to a young child because she believes that once small cuts are covered up, they are gone. Parents can make Band-Aids easily accessible and should let their child wear one whenever she thinks she needs it, even if she just wants to cover an old scab she has rediscovered—the comfort is worth the small expense.

Just as children react in different ways to injuries, so do parents. Some parents minimize their child's pain and say, "You're OK. Stop crying." Other parents offer to rub or kiss the sore spot. Certainly children need comfort when they are upset after a fall, and they need to know their parents understand: "Yes, I know it really hurts when you scrape your knee." But children get hurt so frequently that it can be hard for parents constantly to comfort and reassure. Yet some young children seem to need attention for each new cut, bump, or bruise.

Parents should try not to overreact to their child's injuries. Some parents, who usually realize they are overreacting but have trouble controlling their impulses, rush to their child after a fall, anxiously asking, "Are you all right?" When a child sees her parents looking so concerned, she may start to cry simply because she thinks something must be wrong. If parents continually overreact, their child may eventually feel that she is incapable of making herself feel better, and that she should seek help for even minor accidents.

Some parents are very uncomfortable seeing their son cry after a fall. They may tell him, "You're a big boy, you can handle it. It's only a little cut." Even now, when our society is moving away from stereotyped reactions based on gender, there are parents who think it is all right for girls, but not for boys, to cry. Parents should remember that young children of both sexes sometimes need comfort and sometimes need to handle minor injuries on their own.

When you watch your child playing, you probably warn her about dangerous situations. "Don't climb up there or you'll fall!" If your child climbs and falls anyway, you may have a hard time being sympathetic. It is tempting to say, "I told you

you'd get hurt if you played like that," but if your child is in need of comfort, she will feel rejected by such a statement and not understand the safety message you intend. In such a situation, you should pay attention to your child's pain while also telling her that what she did was unsafe.

On rare occasions, your child's injury may be serious enough for a trip to the doctor or the hospital. A serious accident is always frightening for parents and children, especially if there is a great deal of rush and concern. If your child needs special treatment, reassure her and let her know you understand her pain. "I know your arm hurts and I'm going to see what we can do to make you feel better. That's why we're going to the hospital."

Try to remain calm and explain the medical procedures to your child. Let her know if she will be put on a stretcher or in a papoose, and if a particular procedure will be painful. You and your child may not be able to avoid pain and unpleasantness in this situation, but you can be there to help her and you can go with her to the treatment room if the doctors permit.

It is always hard to see your child in pain after a serious accident, and you might feel better if you bring someone along to help and comfort you—a friend, neighbor, or relative. As one mother said after her daughter received stitches, "I hear about this happening to other children, but it is very different when it happens to your own."

What Do I Do About Climbing?

After a child has been walking for a month or so, she will probably start climbing on chairs, tables, beds, couches, counters, and anything else she can reach. A child climbs because she has a strong urge to touch and explore things around her. When she sees her parents doing seemingly magical things like talking on the phone, washing dishes, turning on lights, or opening doors, she wants to get closer and imitate them. And in order to do that—to reach the phone or the desktop—she has to climb.

The climbing stage can be difficult for parents because they have to keep their child safe, and that can mean almost constant supervision. If parents leave a child alone for even a few moments, they may hear the sound of a chair scraping along as she prepares for her next climb. Parents often stop their child from climbing because they fear for her safety, or because furniture might be damaged, or simply because they don't want her to climb just then. But the child's urge to climb is strong and she may get angry and frustrated when she is held back. Then her parents will either have to deal with her behavior or try to distract her.

A child who climbs during the day may climb out of her crib at night or at naptime, either to be with her parents or to explore the room. Parents are often surprised the first time this happens. One mother put her child in the crib for a nap, then went to take a shower. As she was lathering her hair, she heard a noise in the bathroom and looked out to see her daughter standing there.

It is almost impossible to force your child to stay in her crib, but you can take precautions to make her climbing safer. If your child is consistently climbing out of her crib, clear the nearby area and be sure there are no toys or pieces of furniture for her to trip or fall on. Close the stairway gates whenever she is in her crib, and use a nightlight in the hall so your child can see if she climbs out during the night. If you feel your child is ready, you might want to put the crib away and have her sleep in a bed.

To keep your child safe and satisfied during the day, try at times to make climbing easy for her. You might give her a small stepstool to carry around, or get a small piece of indoor climbing equipment, such as a slide, for her to play on safely. You can also place a chair near a window so she can look out, take cushions off your couch so she can climb on them, or even put a mattress on the floor so your child can climb, jump, and explore in safety.

How Much Childproofing
Should I Do?

Childproofing the home is important because young children explore indiscriminately. If an object is within reach, a child under 3 will touch it without considering his own safety or the value of the object. Because young children have such a strong natural compulsion to touch, see, and explore, their parents have to protect them and make their environment safe. But parents also have to balance their childproofing with an understanding of their child's need to explore.

Most parents know to put plugs in electrical sockets, to put locks on cabinets containing dangerous substances, to keep plants and sharp items out of reach, and to put away valuables. But beyond that, parents wonder how much accommodating they should do. Some parents feel they should teach their child the meaning of "no" by leaving out objects that their child is not allowed to handle. "Sooner or later, he's going to have to learn not to touch everything." Other parents leave out forbidden objects or refuse to let their child touch accessible items in order to train the child to behave well in other people's homes. One mother, who wouldn't let her son play behind the living room curtains, said, "I don't care about my own curtains, but I'm afraid he'll play with the curtains at his friend's house. He might ruin them." Such fears prevent many parents from allowing their child to explore his own house. Yet children can be allowed to touch and play with things at home and taught not to do the same thing at other people's homes.

Parents who leave out knickknacks and declare many items and appliances untouchable, find themselves in constant conflict with their young child, who simply does not have the impulse control to resist touching. One common battleground is the kitchen. Frustrated parents who do not understand the developmental urge to explore, sometimes try to limit their child's access to the dishwasher, trashcan, and refrigerator by tying up doors and lids. Yet such denial may only make a child more frantic to experiment with the interesting appliances he sees his parents use. He may run to the kitchen every time he hears the refrigerator open, or he may struggle to climb on the dishwasher door to get at the silverware. He just wants to touch, but parents often expect too much from a child under 3 and then feel drained from having to say "no" all day.

It's certainly true that a child needs limits, but he will inevitably learn his limitations because there are dangerous and valuable objects that can't be put away: a fireplace, lamps, TV, stereo, etc. There is no need intentionally to leave out other forbidden things, just as there is no need automatically to declare all appliances off-limits. The dishwasher, for instance, won't need to be tied up if parents keep some spoons and plastic dishes and cups within their child's reach inside and let him occasionally practice taking them out and putting them back. Likewise, if parents put some healthy snacks on the bottom shelf of the refrigerator, their child will probably feel satisfied to help himself to those without feeling a need to touch everything else in the refrigerator. If parents are firm about not letting their child handle a few items, but otherwise allow their child freedom to touch, both child and parents will not be overly frustrated during this developmental stage. The more freedom the child has, the more likely he will be to listen when parents tell him not to touch.

Once you have fully childproofed your home, you will feel

comfortable leaving your child alone in one room for a brief time while you work or answer the phone in another room. If you have limited the number of objects your child may not touch, you won't feel tense when he explores. However, expect to keep reminding him of his limits; his urge to touch is so strong that he may not be able to stop himself.

If you want to keep your child from touching things at someone else's house, try telling him ahead of time. "I know you play with the cushions here, but when we're at Grandma's you may not do that." You might find that your child is more cautious when he is away from home, and that he does less exploring in other people's homes than you expected.

Whenever you visit, you may have to do some temporary childproofing, especially if your host has no young children. Ask if you can temporarily move fragile items. Most people will understand, especially if you offer to put the objects back in place before you leave.

Childproofing is basically a way of accommodating the normal developmental needs of a child under 3. Young children want to touch and try everything; if you prepare for this stage you will have an easier time getting through it. And although it may seem to you that the touching phase will never end, you will see a gradual decrease in your child's need to explore everything in sight. By the time he is 3 to 3½, he will gain more understanding about objects, safety, and impulse control and have less need to touch everything. You will then be able to put back on your tables and shelves many of the objects you had to keep out of reach.

In Stores My Child Wants to Touch Everything

Everyone likes to touch interesting and attractive objects. Adults in stores are drawn to gadgets they can manipulate and products they can pick up and feel. Children also want to handle what they see in stores, but many store owners and parents are too impatient or fearful to let children touch.

Yet touching is one of the main ways a child learns about things around her, especially in new surroundings. A child explores with her hands and often can only "see" something by feeling it. One 3-year-old told her mother, who was holding an interesting object right in front of her daughter's eyes, "I can't see that far." The child was really saying that she wanted to touch.

When children shop with their parents, struggles often develop when parents pick up, handle, and buy items, and children want to do the same. And because most stores try to display their products in the most attractive and appealing ways possible, the temptations for a child to touch are great. Parents usually keep their children from handling merchandise because they are worried about items getting broken. While it is true that young children don't understand the consequences of breaking things, it is also true that most children, if properly supervised, won't hurt items in a store. Parents can hold fragile objects for close-up viewing or gentle touching, and can allow their children, within limits, to pick up interesting things.

Sometimes a child will feel satisfied in a store if she is just given enough time to examine an object. Parents are often in too much of a hurry while shopping to wait while their child looks at boxes of nails or piles of scarves. But many struggles can be avoided if parents slow down a bit and allow an extra few minutes for their child's interests.

Some stores make shopping easier by providing toys and play areas for children. If possible, try to patronize such stores and let the owners know that you value their service. Always support their efforts by watching your child while she is in the play area, and by straightening up some of the toys before you leave the store. If children are left unsupervised and if store employees have to take complete responsibility for the play area, owners may discontinue the service.

Although play areas are very helpful, most of the stores you shop in will not have them and will show little tolerance for children. Since that is the case, you may want to carry paper and pens or a toy from home when you shop with your child, or have her bring a backpack with her choice of a few small toys. Such playthings may distract her from some, but not all, of the attractive merchandise around her. When parents, store owners, and employees recognize and become more patient with children's needs to see, touch, and explore, shopping will become an easier task for everyone.

"I Want to Do It Myself!"

Children want to try doing many things for themselves. An 18-month-old wants to push buttons, put a key in the keyhole, walk down the steps, and get his own vitamin. A 2-year-old wants to take the wrapper off his candy and fasten his seatbelt, while a 3-year-old wants to tie his shoes and pour his own juice. Sometimes children are successful at the tasks they choose for themselves, and at other times they struggle in frustration because they lack skills and dexterity. Still, the drive to do for themselves is very strong in young children.

Parents who respect their child's desire to do things for himself help him develop a strong sense of autonomy. Since his self-image is partly determined by the way his parents respond to his desire for independence, he will feel good about himself when he is allowed to tackle jobs on his own. On the other hand, if his parents discourage him too often from trying to help himself, he will begin to doubt his own abilities.

In general, parents should let their child at least start a task he's interested in. If he is unsuccessful, they can offer guidance, and if he is unable to follow their suggestions they can then offer to do the job for him. Parents often jump in too soon because they find it difficult to watch their child struggle with a task. Parents naturally want to help, but often their child doesn't want help. If parents find it too hard to stay uninvolved, they should occupy themselves with something else while their child works.

At times, such as when a family is out in public, parents will not be able to let their child do a task for himself. One family, for example, was about to go home after seeing a circus when their 2-year-old insisted on tying his own shoe. As they tried to help him and hurry him along, he became angry and frustrated, and nearby families stopped to watch the struggle: "No, I want to do it myself!" The parents finally solved the problem by telling their son he could carry his shoe out and tie it himself in the car, but often such conflicts are not easily resolved.

Despite the best intentions, parents may find themselves in an embarrassing situation, carrying away a screaming, angry child who wants to stay put until he has finished a task. Such times are difficult for parents, who feel judged by others and frustrated by their child's actions. Yet the child doesn't understand his parents' feelings, and will often focus only on his own needs unless he is distracted.

Sometimes parents don't want their child to do a job for himself because they don't want to deal with the mess that will result, or because they are in a hurry. But when parents say, "Let me do that for you," they may be in for arguments, struggles, or temper tantrums.

To minimize such resistance, warn your child ahead of time if there will not be time for him to dress himself or do some other task: "We are in a hurry today, so I'm going to help you." Try to distract him: "Why don't you look at this book while I put your shoes on?" "Let me tell you a story while I get your breakfast ready."

If a task your child wants to try is too difficult or messy, break it into steps and let your child try a small part of the job. If he can't yet brush his teeth, let him hold the toothbrush while you put the toothpaste on, and let him hold your hand as you brush.

He will feel pleased to participate, and in time, step by step, he will take over the job for himself.

Being patient with children at this stage is difficult, because at times patience, distraction, and preparation do not work— your child will angrily demand to do something for himself when you don't want him to, or when he is incapable of doing the job. Still, the more your child is allowed to try on his own, the less likely he is to argue when you have to take over a task. And as you see how pleased your child is with his accomplishments and how good he feels about his abilities, you will understand why it is important to let him do many things for himself.

My Child Wants
to Dress Herself

All young children have a strong need to do things for themselves, and one of the first tasks most children try is getting dressed on their own. Children feel proud and excited when they dress themselves, and they look to their parents for approval.

There is no need to try convincing or teaching a young child to dress herself, because most children express an interest in the activity on their own. First a child will learn to take off her shoes, socks, and pants, since children are able to take their clothes off before they can put them on. By age 3, the child may want to do most of her own dressing (excluding snaps and buttons), although her clothes will often be inside out or backwards. By the time she is 4 or 5, she will be able to dress herself completely with little help.

When your child begins dressing herself, she may be frustrated by zippers, snaps, buttons, and shirts with small neck openings. Even though she cannot master these, she may insist on trying—a situation that often leads to anger and tantrums. You might want to avoid difficult clothes and buy pull-on pants and tops until your child is ready to use fasteners.

As your child learns to dress herself, she may want to practice her new skills by changing her clothes several times a day, creating great piles of clothing to clean up or launder. She may also want to choose her own clothes, sometimes picking the same easy-to-put-on outfit over and over, or choosing clothes that don't fit well, don't match, or are inappropriate for the weather or the occasion. As long as you are staying inside, there's no need to make an issue out of how she looks. But at times when you want your child to look nice, you may end up struggling over her choice of clothes.

You can eliminate some of the problem by laying out two outfits and letting your child choose one to wear, or by putting in your child's drawers only those clothes that fit and are suitable for the season. Another possibility is to fill one drawer with a few sets of clothes that mix and match, letting your child choose what to wear from these pre-selected outfits. These suggestions require time and energy, but the effort might be worth it if your child is determined to pick out her own clothes each day.

When you are rushed, you may end up struggling with your child if she is determined to dress herself. If you leave the house every morning, you may be able to avoid arguments by setting the alarm clock 15 minutes early to give your child time to dress. At other times, you may have to let her know that you are going to help with dressing because you are rushed. If she has generally been allowed to dress herself, she may not resist your efforts. But if she does, try saying, "Let's get dressed quickly so we can get some crackers or have time to play."

A surprising development may occur once your child has learned to dress herself efficiently: she may not want to do it anymore. She may say, "I can't," or "I don't want to," or "You get me dressed." Frequently, when a child has mastered a skill such as dressing, she loses interest in it and it becomes a chore rather than a challenge. You may feel that if you give in and dress your child, you are being manipulated. You may even try to force her to dress herself although when children are forced, they often slow down and procrastinate. You have to decide whether this is an issue worth struggling over.

Compromise and flexibility seem most effective. If your child is tired or uninterested, or simply wants to be taken care of for a while, it is all right to dress her yourself. At other times you may want to help her get dressed: "You do the shirt and I'll put on your pants." And when you want her to dress herself, usually by the time she is 5, let her know: "Before you come down for breakfast I want you to get dressed."

It is best to avoid power struggles over getting dressed. In child development, it is common that steps forward are often followed by steps backward. Enjoy your child's pride when she is able to dress herself, and trust that by age 5 or 6 she will take the job on permanently.

When Will My Child Be Ready to Use the Toilet?

The transition from diapers to toilet use is an important one in a child's development. If parents are patient and non-pressuring as their child learns to use the toilet, the family will get through this stage easily. But if parents try to force toilet training, this stage may cause a lot of anger and unhappiness.

Parents often initiate early toilet training because they feel a great deal of pressure. Nursery schools and day care centers want children to be trained, and friends and relatives offer criticism: "You were trained at 2! What's wrong with your child?" "You really should start toilet training him." There is often competition among parents to see who has the youngest toilet trained child, as though toilet training were a race. Many people mistakenly feel that the faster a child develops (and the sooner he is toilet trained), the smarter or better he is.

Aside from starting toilet training in response to pressure, many parents start because they don't believe their child will learn the skill on his own. Although parents have seen their child teach himself to crawl, walk, and talk, they find it hard to trust that he will also use the toilet when he's ready.

Children can train themselves, but the ages at which they are able to do so vary since in this, as in all areas of development, some children are ready sooner than others. Between 2½ and 3, most children gain enough bladder and bowel control to be able to use the toilet on their own, although some children do not use the toilet until they are 3½. Emotional factors such as the birth of a sibling, a move, or the start of school can delay a child's readiness to use the toilet.

Often, children show an interest in the toilet at 18 months, but parents should not take this as a sign that a child is ready for toilet training. At this age a child's body is not mature enough and any toilet use will be controlled by his parents; he is just temporarily interested in flushing the toilet, tearing toilet paper, and imitating the other members of his family. Many children under 2 are afraid of the toilet. It is large, and they fear they will fall in or be flushed down and disappear. A small potty seat is less frightening, but many children won't use one, insisting on using the same toilet the rest of the family uses.

If parents initiate toilet training before their child is ready, the whole family may suffer. Parents use up a great deal of energy putting a child on the toilet every 20 minutes; constantly praising, questioning, or scolding him; doing the extra laundry and cleanup that results from frequent accidents; and working out reward systems using candy or stars to motivate their child. It is particularly difficult for parents to handle the resistance of a 2-year-old who reacts negatively to any parental pressure or suggestions. At that age, a child strives for autonomy and wants to assert himself and take charge of all aspects of his life: "I want to do it myself!" Certainly there are some children who are easily trained by their parents, and other children who quickly learn to use the toilet because they temporarily fear losing their parents' love and acceptance. But most children are not successfully toilet trained when their parents start too soon.

Often, all of the parental training efforts backfire, and the child becomes strongly opposed to using the toilet. This situation can develop because a child has been over-praised for toilet use. Once the child sees how important the issue is to his parents and how happy they are when he goes to the bathroom, he realizes on some level how unhappy he can make them by not going. This may become his weapon in power struggles.

Toilet training efforts can also backfire because a child has been pressed too hard to be "a big boy." Sometimes a child feels so anxious about disappointing his parents that he won't even try using the toilet for fear of failure. Finally, a child who does not like to be pushed and controlled might try to exert his own power by rejecting his parents' suggestions. Rather than use the toilet, he might become constipated or else urinate or have a bowel movement as soon as he is taken off the toilet, soiling the floor or his pants. If parents feel they must initiate toilet training before their child is ready, they should hold off until he is 3 and make sure training does not interfere with other developmental changes.

However, the best approach to toilet training is to wait until the child is ready to start using the toilet on his own. Children have an innate drive to grow and develop, and a strong desire to imitate their parents, to please their parents, and to do things for themselves. All of these urges will come together if the child is not pressured to use the toilet before he is physically and emotionally ready. It takes a great deal of patience and confidence in your child to wait for him to show he is ready. But eventually he will let you know that he wants to use the toilet. Offer support and help: "Would you like me to turn on the light? Can I help you with your pants?" You can give simple acknowledgment of what your child has done, or you might want to reflect back to him his own pleasure and pride.

Once your child has initiated toilet use on his own, he will quickly give up diapers. However, even past 4 years old, he will occasionally have accidents because of stress or he will forget, because he will be too busy playing, to get to a bathroom on time. As long as you have not excessively praised him or excessively shamed him for his previous toilet use and accidents, he will not feel too bad when he wets.

Your attitudes towards toilet training determine, in large part, how successful this phase of your child's development will be. If you anticipate struggles, you will probably have struggles over toilet use. But if you are relaxed and willing to let your child set the pace, you and he will have an easier time.

SETTING LIMITS

How Do I Handle Discipline and Punishment?

Parents often feel they spend a great part of each day disciplining their young children: "Don't use the toy that way—you might hurt someone," "No hitting," "Leave the dog alone," "You have to come in now," "That's too loud." Setting limits for young children can be a difficult, complex, time-consuming task, but one that is essential. Parents have to teach their child acceptable behavior, while controlling or changing her unacceptable behavior until she is old enough to exert some self-control. In order to handle this task effectively, parents need an understanding of their child's developmental stages, realistic expectations, empathy, patience, and love and respect for their child.

Disciplining young children is an extremely important part of parenting, yet there are parents who don't set limits or who do so inadequately. Some parents feel overwhelmed by their child's behavior and may not know "where to start." Other parents just don't think about the importance of setting limits or else leave the job to others—neighbors, friends, relatives, and most commonly, teachers. Probably the major reason parents fail to discipline their child is because they fear her anger and the loss of her love. Rather than face rejection from their child, they ignore her unacceptable behavior, give in to her, or rationalize: "Kids will be kids." But setting consistent limits is one of the major responsibilities of parenting and not a job that should be ignored or put off.

Many parents doubt their ability to discipline: "Am I too strict? Too lenient? Do I expect too much?" Parents are embarrassed by their child's misbehavior in public and wonder what they've done wrong or why their child seems worse than others. Since a child's behavior is a reflection on her parents, they feel vulnerable and judged by others when their child acts inappropriately; such feelings are normal. Yet parents should realize that misbehavior is a basic part of childhood. A child learns what is correct by trying all sorts of behavior, "good" and "bad," until she finds out what is and isn't acceptable.

Parents should base their expectations and their methods of disciplining on their child's age and ability to understand. A child under 2 needs constant watching and reminding, while a 4- or 5-year-old is developing enough self-control and understanding to have some sense of right and wrong. Methods that work with older children, such as telling a child to spend "time out," or telling her the consequences of her misbehavior, are ineffective with younger children who do not understand or remember the rules they're told.

Children 3 and younger have such strong developmental needs to explore, touch, and do things for themselves, that they have difficulty sticking to limits. Because their immediate needs are so great and because they focus so completely on the here and now, they often don't realize they are doing something wrong, even if they've been told many times. When reprimanded, children this age will often look surprised and hurt.

In order to set limits for a child this age, parents have to stay fairly close by, get involved with their child, and always be aware of what she's doing. When children are not supervised, they lose sight of appropriate boundaries of acceptable and unacceptable behavior. If a child is playing dangerously or inappropriately, her parents have to be right there, gently but firmly correcting her: "No, you can't play that way—it's too dangerous." If talking doesn't work, parents should remove their child from the situation or take away the dangerous object, explain why, and then involve their child in something else: "I'm not going to let you climb over that chair because you might fall, but you can play here on the cushions." Sometimes offering an alternative works because children can be easily distracted by interesting objects and activities. Connecting a restriction to an activity also works because a young child can understand the relationship: "If you want to ride your bike, you have to stay in front of the house," "If you want to play outside, you have to keep your jacket on."

Children 3 and under often reject limits and say "no," not only because they want to continue their activities, but because they are asserting their independence and learning what they can do. And sometimes parents set limits unnecessarily because they underestimate what a young child can do. One 3-year-old, who wanted to hold a screwdriver, was told, "No, it's too dangerous." But when the child protested, her father decided to let her try as long as she sat at a table next to him so he could supervise. The child was happy, and her father realized that he could relax some of the limitations he had set.

Usually, though, parents know how they want their child to act. When a child misbehaves, parents often feel angry and momentarily withdraw their love and attention from the child. Since a young child wants parental approval, she feels hurt when she is criticized for doing something wrong. She can't separate her action from herself and feels that she is being rejected for who she is, not for what she has done. The removal of parental acceptance often motivates a 2- or 3-year-old to change her behavior and to run to her parents for a hug after she's been disciplined.

A 4- or 5-year-old may not react this way. After being disciplined, her hurt feelings and embarrassment might turn to anger and resistance, and she may test her own power and her parents' limits. Yet she too wants to be loved and accepted, and finds parental approval a strong motivator.

Verbal limit setting and distraction work with 4- and 5-year-olds, but since they have a better understanding of consequences than younger children do, they also respond to other methods of disciplining. When a 4-year-old becomes angry and aggressive, her parents can first try to reason with her or distract her. If she doesn't calm down, they can say, "Your behavior is unacceptable. If you continue acting this way you will need to spend time in your room. When you change your behavior you can join us." If parents have to follow through on this, they can tell their child she can come out of her room as soon as she is in control of herself.

It is better, in such a situation, to let the child determine the amount of time she will spend in her room. When parents set a limit, but not a time limit, the cooling off period lasts only as long as is necessary for the child to calm down. If instead parents dictate a waiting period of 20 minutes or half an hour, the child may calm down and then forget why she was sent to her room as she involves herself with her toys and books. Even 15 minutes of isolation is a long time unless the choice to stay away is the child's. The point of taking time out is not to spend time away from the family, but to change unacceptable behavior. However, if the child abuses the right to set her own time-out period or if her behavior remains unchanged, her parents should set a time limit themselves.

Many times, parents punish children by taking away toys or privileges. This can be effective as long as there is a connection between the child's misbehavior and what's taken away. For instance, if a child uses her bike in a dangerous way, an appropriate consequence would be for her parents temporarily to take away the bike. A child who continually throws sand would lose the privilege of playing in the sandbox for an afternoon.

Before taking something away, parents should warn their child about what will happen if she continues to misbehave. And the object or privilege should not be removed for an excessively long time or the child will concentrate only on the unfairness of the situation, not on her misbehavior. The point of this punishment is to help the child think about her own behavior and see a logical connection between, for instance, abusing the bike and losing the bike. Often the warning that there will be consequences is enough to deter a child from misbehaving again.

Although it is best that the lost toy or privilege be connected in some way to the negative behavior, it is not always possible for parents to find a connection. If a child hits her brother, what should her parents take away? In such cases, parents sometimes remove something unrelated, such as a toy or dessert. Although it is unwise to make dessert a focus of power, many parents find that their child changes her behavior when threatened with the loss of sweets for a meal.

When taking something away, or using any other form of punishment, parents should be sure the consequences come soon after the child's misbehavior. This gives the child a chance to connect her actions with their consequences, and it ensures that parents will follow through. Often, when parents tell a child in the morning that she will be punished in the evening, the child knows that her parents may forget or change their minds.

One mother, eating lunch in a fast food restaurant with her child, said, "If you keep misbehaving you're going to bed at 7:00 tonight." When the child continued acting up the mother said, "All right. Now you're going to bed at 6:30." The punishment seemed so far away and so drastic to the child that she felt helpless and continued misbehaving. Instead of making a distant threat, the mother could have tried distracting her daughter or telling her she would have to move to the next table, or warning her they would have to leave the restaurant. Then the child could have made the connection between her inappropriate behavior and the consequences.

A disciplining method that some parents find successful is counting: "By the time I count to 5, I want you indoors," or "I'll count to 10 while you get ready for your bath." This usually offers the child a limit, a warning, and a bit of time, although if the technique is overused it becomes ineffective.

An important element of disciplining a child of any age is the tone of voice parents use. When parents sound firm and sure of themselves, children often respond well; but when parents are unsure about what limits to impose, their children get mixed messages. The most effective tone is respectful but firm. Parents should begin setting a limit by speaking in a quiet, polite, firm voice. If that doesn't work, they can assert themselves more forcefully and speak in an authoritarian voice. But yelling at a child is not as effective as firmly stating a limit (although it is often difficult to keep from yelling). It is sometimes helpful to stand close to a child, quietly repeating a warning or prohibition.

When disciplining a child, parents should always consider their own anger. Sometimes, when parents are bothered by personal problems, they overreact to their child's misbehavior. Parents should let their child know when they are in bad moods and at some point apologize if they have been unreasonably harsh. When parents feel out of control and unable to deal with their anger, they should spend time in a separate room away from their child until they calm down.

It is important that parents not be too forceful and harsh when disciplining their child. If the child always loses, or is always given negative feedback and doesn't feel accepted, what incentive does she have to behave well? Parents who are too hard on their child only encourage her anger and aggression, while causing her to feel bad about herself.

It may be helpful for parents to remember their own feelings as children. Were they disciplined harshly? Do they want their child to know the same anger and frustration they once experienced? Parents who felt unfairly disciplined often say they will not treat their child the same way, but in moments of anger, it takes a great deal of patience to deal with a young child's inappropriate behavior in appropriate ways.

As you discipline your child, remember that children learn not just from your words, but from your actions. If you treat your child with kindness and respect and show her that you value her, she will model her behavior after yours. When children feel good, they usually behave nicely and have an easier time accepting the limits you impose. And when children are treated courteously, they learn what courteous behavior is. It is as important to praise and encourage your child when you are pleased with her as it is to set limits when you are unhappy.

It takes time and patience to help children learn self-discipline. If you have tried everything you can and your child still acts inappropriately at an age when she should have learned a fair amount of control, see if something is disturbing your family relationship. The birth of a baby, a move, family illness, fighting between parents, divorce, etc., can cause behavior problems. Usually such problems are temporary, but if they persist, you should consider seeking professional advice on how to discipline and help your child.

What Should I Do About Temper Tantrums?

"I want this now!" shouts a 3-year-old, pulling candy off a grocery shelf.

"Not today," says his mother.

"Yes, I want candy!"

When his mother again refuses, the child responds with a full-fledged temper tantrum: screaming, crying, thrashing, and kicking. Tantrums like this are hard to watch, they are embarrassing, and they can make parents feel helpless.

Why do children have tantrums? The answers are rooted in the developmental characteristics of young children. These children have very little self-control; they live in the here and now, and try to act on their immediate desires. When parents respond to a child's wishes by saying "no," the child reacts negatively, sometimes sensing rejection. Young children lack the ability to think logically and follow adult reasoning. A child will probably not understand why his parents deny one of his wishes, even though their explanations may make perfect sense. Another reason for temper tantrums, particularly with pre-verbal toddlers, is the young child's inability to express his needs and wants fully. When a child's parents can't understand him he becomes easily frustrated and may express his feelings by having a tantrum.

If you are concerned about temper tantrums, there are a number of approaches you can try, including prevention. Since you know your child's wants, you can guess which situations are likely to cause tantrums, and by planning ahead for these times, you may be able to avoid a problem. For example, when you anticipate a struggle at the candy counter, carry a few small toys, some juice, or some crackers with you. If the situation becomes tense, you can use these to distract your child.

If you are anticipating a struggle when you shop with your 3- or 4-year-old, set limits before you enter the store. You can say, "We're only looking today. I'm not going to buy you anything," or "Remember, I'm only buying you one thing." Try to be sure your child understands the limits before you enter the store. But remember, it is hard for a child to "only look" and not buy.

There is another technique that may prevent a tantrum: compromise. You can tell your child, "I won't buy candy, but I will buy you a pretzel." This and the other prevention methods sometimes work well, but at times your child may have a temper tantrum in spite of your efforts. If this happens, you'll have to decide how to respond to your child. Most likely your reaction will vary with the situation, depending on where you are and whom you are with. But your choices will be the same—you can meet your child's demand, distract your child, or let him have the tantrum.

You may choose to meet your child's demand because you realize that it is not so unreasonable after all. Perhaps you were being too rigid when you first rejected his request. Or perhaps you feel that saying "no" to his desire is not worth the struggle or tantrum.

If you don't give in to your child, you may try distracting him. Remind your child about a recent pleasurable experience, point out something interesting, or talk about something good that will happen soon. You may be surprised at how effective distraction can be in defusing a conflict.

Finally, you may choose to let your child's tantrum run its course. Although coping can be hard, if you try to wait calmly and ignore the tantrum, your child will soon quiet down. Just be sure he is safe during his tantrum and unable to harm another person or an object.

Tantrums are difficult for you and your young child. But as your child grows older he will gain more understanding and you will find it easier to set limits. Once he outgrows that urgent need to have everything NOW, there will be far fewer tantrums to struggle with.

Does Spanking Really Help?

Parents spank their child when they are angry and frustrated or when they don't know how else to get their point across. For many parents, spanking seems the only way to teach children to listen and behave well. Yet spanking is not necessary; there are other, more effective ways to get children to change their behavior.

In our society, spanking is a widely accepted method of discipline. Although many parents defend spanking by saying, "I was spanked and I turned out OK," or "It's the only way to get the message across," other parents feel guilty, defensive, and embarrassed about hitting their children. "I know I shouldn't have spanked him, but . . ." Parents often wince when seeing a child spanked in public and wonder, "Is that what I do to my child?" Some parents feel guilty after spanking and want to follow up with a hug or an apology to assure themselves they have not lost their child's love. Still other parents say that though they spank, they really don't believe spanking changes their child's negative behavior. Even those parents who strongly believe in the effectiveness of spanking say it usually only temporarily stops inappropriate behavior.

There are problems with spanking. One is that a child will imitate what her parents do. If her parents hit her in order to change her behavior, why shouldn't she also hit when someone does something she doesn't like? Can parents fairly tell their child not to hit when they discipline her by spanking?

Spanking can be a particular problem with a child under 2½, who often does not understand ahead of time that an action is wrong. A small child may touch a glass vase because she thinks it is beautiful. If she is suddenly spanked, she won't easily understand that she has done something inappropriate, but rather will focus on the pain and shock of the spanking. It is very difficult for a child this age to make a connection between her own behavior and a spanking, yet one of the goals of discipline is to have children make those connections.

Spanking a child who is over 3 may actually hinder discipline. Parents hope their child will eventually develop self-discipline and a sense of right and wrong. As the child grows older, she should begin to feel bad about her unacceptable behavior, and her guilt should keep her from behaving in the same inappropriate ways again. But when the child is spanked for her wrongdoings, she does not learn to monitor her own behavior. She may learn instead that as long as she does not get caught, she can misbehave. And if she does get caught, any guilt feelings she has will be relieved by the spanking, since she has "paid the consequences." Eventually the child will learn that if she can tolerate the spanking, she no longer has to feel bad about her negative actions or try to alter her behavior. She can do what she wants, get spanked, and then be free to do what she wants again. Even when parents explain to the child why they have spanked her and how they want her to change, the child may be too angry or humiliated at the time of the spanking to listen and learn.

Discipline works best when parents set firm limits verbally and then follow through by removing their child from the scene of her misbehavior, taking away an object or privilege she has abused, or having her spend time alone until she can change her behavior. When punishment is relevant to the inappropriate behavior—when the child who throws a block has to stop playing with the blocks—the child can make the connection between her action and its consequences. Until children develop self-control, they are motivated best by the desire for parental approval, and by the fear of losing privileges and toys.

Even a child under 2 can make a connection when she is given a firm "no" and removed from a dangerous or inappropriate situation. Parents often feel that they must spank their young child to teach her critical safety rules such as not to play in the street. But firm and consistent warnings, frequent reminders, and close supervision are effective in keeping children out of danger.

Sometimes parents say, "When I tell my child to stop, she ignores me, but when I spank her, she does what I want." One mother, who was browsing in a department store with her 2-year-old, became angry when her son tried to investigate the dressing rooms. She repeatedly warned him not to go near them and then spanked him for not listening. The child cried, turned around in circles several times and looked defeated. The situation is a familiar one, yet the mother had other options that would have left her and her child feeling happier. Since young children have a hard time listening to limits when they have an intense need to explore, the mother could have acknowledged her child's interest and even taken a moment to look into the dressing room with him. This might have made it easier for him to do what his mother wanted. Or she could have gently but firmly told him there was no time to explore that day. She could also have tried to distract him, or to carry him away from the area of the dressing room.

Disciplining children is a complex, gradual task. Your young child needs to be reminded of her limits over and over, and you will have to be patient as she slowly learns self-discipline. If you spank your child in an effort to discipline her, she will feel defenseless, humiliated, and angry, and may not understand the connection between what she did and what you are doing to her. It takes a lot of self-control not to spank and to trust that your child can learn appropriate behavior without being spanked. If, instead of spanking your child, you set firm limits and follow through in relevant ways, your child will be able to listen to you without feeling vulnerable and defeated.

Must I Always Be Consistent?

Parents often wonder how important it is to be consistent when setting limits for their child. Should parents stick with a rule in order to help their child learn what is expected of him? Does consistency teach the child that he can't always have his way? Will bending the rules harm the child or cause his parents to lose control?

When parents are consistent, they provide their child with a sense of what is and isn't acceptable behavior. And in some areas, such as vital safety rules, consistency is essential. Yet if parents tried to enforce consistently every rule they set, they would spend all of their time saying, "No, don't do that," and "No, you can't have that." Every parent makes exceptions to the rules, depending on circumstance and personality. Some parents are quite flexible, others generally inflexible. Yet most find themselves at some point saying, "No, not today," then changing that to, "Maybe," and finally saying, "OK, you can."

One father took his daughter to a convenience store. The girl said, "I want a Coke," but her father replied in a firm but gentle voice, "I am only going in this store for milk and eggs." The girl said, "But I want one Coke for me." The father said, "I'm not buying you a Coke, but I will give you a drink when we get home." Minutes later the father and daughter walked out of the store. The father held his bag of eggs and milk and his daughter walked out with a Coke—with a straw in it.

Parents often fear that when they give in, their child will expect the same response the next time a similar situation arises. But as long as parents are generally firm about discipline, they can make exceptions and still stay in control. When parents show some flexibility, they let their child know that his desires are important, and that life is not too rigid. He learns that sometimes people get what they want, and sometimes they don't, and he learns what compromise feels like. And he has the experience of occasionally winning a struggle with his parents. It is all right to let a child win sometimes, especially when sticking to a particular rule is not worth the parents' effort.

You probably find that time, place, and mood influence your decision to stick to a rule or give in. Sometimes you feel tolerant, sometimes you are impatient, sometimes you feel tired and don't want a struggle, and sometimes you are out in public and don't want to be embarrassed. You may be more likely to give in when you need to distract your child because you are working or talking on the phone.

One mother would not generally let her son mix spices and water together in a bowl as he had done with great enjoyment at a friend's house. But her son learned a way around the prohibition. Whenever his mother took a business call, the boy would start getting spices off the shelf, usually with his mother's reluctant help. She needed to keep him quiet when she was on the phone and so gave in and let him play his mixing game.

If you are concerned about being consistent, consider your overall relationship with your child. If you generally give the message that your child is loved, cared for, and accepted, and that you have basic, firm expectations about how he should behave, you don't have to worry about the incidental exceptions you make. Being reasonably consistent is good enough. After all, you cannot enforce a set of rules at all times. Flexibility is an important part of life, and give and take is an important part of parenting.

Can Too Much Praise Backfire?

To many people, praise seems like a wonderful tool to use with children. Praising children is one way to help them feel good about themselves, and praise motivates children to do what pleases their parents. Yet too much praise, even when delivered with the best of intentions, can have a negative impact.

A young child has strong inner drives to accomplish things for herself and to succeed at many tasks. She is excited about learning, motivated to try new things, and eager to imitate adults. Parents can tell how proud their child is when she says, "Look, I got my shirt on by myself," or "I know how to count to 10." The child's reward for these achievements is her own sense of accomplishment.

When parents offer moderate praise for these achievements and reflect their child's own excitement ("I can see how happy you are," "You seem really excited.") the child knows that her parents are pleased with her behavior. But when parents offer excessive praise ("Great job!" "I'm so proud of you!"), especially for everyday aspects of life such as toilet use or eating, the child may begin to expect such praise for everything she does. Eventually the child may try to achieve not for internal satisfaction, but for the reward of praise, and the child's feelings of accomplishment may become of secondary importance. The child may think, "I'll tie my shoe because Mom will think it's great."

A child who is praised for every achievement may begin to distrust the praise and her own abilities. Is everything she does really that good? Or is anything she does really good at all? The child may become dependent on praise and may not believe she has done something worthwhile unless she hears lavish compliments. Excessive praise can also put pressure on the child. When she is praised so heavily for doing well, she may feel she has to continue achieving or lose the praise and attention. Many parents will understand these negative effects of praise if they consider how dependent they, as adults, are on external praise and rewards.

It is fine to praise your child, and you certainly want to let her know that you feel good about her. But give praise in moderation and try to encourage your child to feel good about her own abilities. Focus on her desire to do things for herself, and praise her by speaking more about her feelings than your own: "You really felt good about climbing that jungle gym, didn't you?" By responding that way, you recognize your child's pride in her success. You can also praise your child effectively in nonverbal ways. A hug, a smile, a look of approval all communicate your good feelings about your child.

"You're a Big Boy Now"
"You're a Big Girl Now"

Parents can often be heard telling their young child to act "bigger." "You're a big boy now, so you should use the toilet," or "You're too big to make such a mess." Parents use "big boy" as a discipline tool and as a way to change their child's behavior, either by appealing to his desire to do what older children do, or by shaming him with a comparison to younger children.

The problem with urging a child to be a "big boy" is that the child, who already wants to act older and more capable, feels pressure from his parents to change and do things he may not be able to do. When he can't act like a "big boy," he may feel bad about parts of himself that he usually can't control and about not being able to please his parents. In a public restroom, a mother changed her son's diaper while telling him, "You're a big boy now. You're too old for diapers." The child looked ashamed. Yet if he had been ready to use the toilet, he would have given up diapers on his own. Exhortations to be "bigger" won't help him—they will only make him feel bad about himself.

In a similar situation, a woman took her grandson to a toy store and asked him to pick something out. When he chose a stuffed animal, she said, "Oh, no. Not that. You're too big to want that." When adults say such things to a child they tell him that his feelings and desires are unacceptable, and that he should be acting differently.

If you think your child is not as "big" as he should be, try to understand why. He might use babytalk or play with a younger child's toys because of a new sibling or the start of a new school. And since each child develops at his own pace, your child may just not be physically ready for the behavior changes you would like to see. By temperament, he may be a child who cries more than other children or who needs more closeness and security than others. Also, children struggle as they grow, and for every step forward, there is usually a short step backward to earlier behavior.

All children have a strong drive to be independent and to imitate older people. If you accept your child as he is and wait patiently without pressuring him, you will see him begin to act "bigger" on his own.

Why Does My Child Bite?

During infancy, children find satisfaction in sucking and biting. They experience pleasure when they suck warm milk from the breast or bottle, and they learn about taste and texture by putting objects in their mouths. Until about 18 months of age, children bite and chew on toys, household objects, and other things they find in their explorations.

Sometimes a baby will bite other people, especially when her gums are sore from teething. Although such a bite can be painful, parents should remember that the child is not intentionally trying to hurt. Occasionally, a very young child may bite her mother during nursing. Mothers may be so alarmed at this that they wonder if they should start weaning, but such a drastic step is not necessary. If the mother takes the breast away from her biting child and says "no" firmly, the child will quickly learn not to bite while nursing.

An infant's innocent biting is very different from the deliberate, frustrated biting of a 2- or 3-year-old. Sometimes a preschooler's anger cannot be expressed through words, and she impulsively bites. Parents of toddlers and young preschoolers who bite don't often feel understanding and accepting about the problem—and rightly so. When a child bites, parents should set firm limits, saying, "I don't want you biting anyone," or "I know you are really angry, but biting is not acceptable," or "You will have to find another way to let me know you are angry," or simply, "I will not allow you to bite." Letting a child know immediately and firmly that biting is unacceptable is important.

If talking doesn't solve the problem, parents of a biting toddler or preschooler should move off a distance from their child, letting her know with a quiet but firm tone that they are angry with her and do not want to be near her when she bites. Parents can also sit their child on a step or in her room for a short while. Since children often change their behavior in order to please their parents, some children will stop biting so they can feel accepted again.

Occasionally you may be tempted to cure your child's biting habit by biting her back to "show her what it feels like." But biting a child back is inappropriate. First, you give a mixed message: you tell your child not to bite, but then do it yourself. Second, your young child has a difficult time putting herself in another person's place, and does not understand that the pain she feels from a bite is the same pain that she inflicts when she bites. You can teach appropriate behavior best by setting limits, being a good model for your child, and showing her how to act in socially acceptable ways.

If your child continually bites, she is probably troubled by something deeper than momentary frustration; in such a case, admonitions and firm limits usually will not work. Since biting is a sign of anger, frustration, and aggression, try to discover the cause of your child's behavior. Perhaps there is tension at home, a new baby, or difficulty in preschool. If you cannot find the cause of continued biting, you may want to seek advice from your pediatrician or mental health professional who can explore possible areas of tension in the family.

Is It All Right to Bribe Children?

"If you . . . then you can . . ." It's a familiar pattern heard when parents try to persuade their child to do something: "If you come with me now, I'll buy you a treat at the grocery." "If you put your toys away, you can stay up 15 minutes later tonight." There are always family struggles about the routines and necessities of life: bedtime, bath time, shopping, leaving a friend's house, getting dressed, getting ready for school, etc. When logic fails (as it often does) and a young child refuses to do what his parents wish, they often resort to bribing.

In theory, most parents are opposed to bribes. Parents want their children to cooperate and to learn to tolerate frustration, and they don't want their children to expect rewards for good behavior. But it takes years for a child to learn self-control and to understand that chores have to be done, even when people don't want to do them. Until a child can motivate himself to do necessary tasks, bribery has its uses, and parents will find that an occasional bribe is a strong motivator. But parents should be careful not to overuse bribes, or children will look for constant rewards.

One mother could not get her son to leave his friend's house, even though it was time for dinner. Finally she said, "If you come home now, you can paint with watercolors after dinner and you can invite David to come over and play tomorrow." After hearing these offers, the boy agreed to leave his friend's house. Another mother wanted to have her child come and play indoors, but the boy refused. However, when the mother said, "Let's go in and I'll play a game with you, and then we'll have a cookie," the child decided to come in. Bribes such as these can distract or redirect a child, and often eliminate struggles and temper tantrums.

Bribes can also be used to avoid embarrassment. When parents are out in public, they may prefer to offer a bribe rather than face a tantrum from a child who resists their plans. When parents go shopping with their child, they may give him a cookie or toy to gain his cooperation and make the shopping trip go smoothly.

You may be worried that once you offer a bribe in a situation, your child will come to expect one whenever a similar situation comes up. But this is rarely a problem, since children can accept compromise and a degree of inconsistency. If you bribed your child to go grocery shopping with you last week, but don't want to offer a bribe this week, let him know ahead of time: "Last time we went shopping I bought you gum, but when we go today I'm not buying a treat." When you get to the store, remind him of your warning, if necessary, and try to distract him: "I like to bring you to the store with me so you can help pick out food for dinner." If you are firm and if you allow occasional compromise, your child will usually cooperate with you.

One way to eliminate the need for frequent bribes is to give your child plenty of warning when you want him to switch activities or to go along with you cooperatively. If he is engrossed in play, tell him, "We need to go to the post office after you're done with your game with Joan." Then remind him 10 minutes before you are ready to leave so he can bring his game to a pleasant, slow close. That way, he won't have to stop abruptly doing what he wants in order to do what you want. And the chances are good that he will come along peacefully, without needing a bribe.

Should I Make My Child
Clean Up?

Trying to clean up after young children is a thankless task. Children pull toys out of closets, drawers, and shelves, and when they're done playing with one thing, they drop it on the floor and get out something new. They also take pots and pans out of cabinets, unroll toilet paper, and leave clothes and shoes lying around. In just a short time, a young child can create a great deal of disorder.

Some of this messiness can be explained. Young children's interests shift quickly from one object to another, so even a brief play period may result in a big pile of toys. And because children like to play wherever their parents are, they carry (and leave) toys all over the house. Taking toys out is fun but picking them up is not.

That job is usually left for parents, and the daily process of putting things away can be both demanding and unrewarding. Many parents want or expect help from their children, but until children reach early elementary age, parents can expect little relief. That's because young children do not think about cleaning up in the same way that adults do. Children are truly unaware of the tasks they leave for their parents.

All parents must decide whether to constantly clean up after their children or let the cleaning go at times so the family can accomplish other things. Of course some adults care more about neatness than others. And some parents fear letting things get too messy because of unexpected visitors or the prospect of large-scale cleanups. Parents who work outside the home may feel a particular desire for a neat house because their cleanup time is so limited.

Although everyone would like help in maintaining a clean home, parents who pressure their young children to clean up may actually stifle the exploration and play that are a necessary part of childhood. For example, a child who is always expected to put her blocks away may lose interest in using the blocks to build. Also, those parents who feel compelled to establish early patterns of cleaning up may find the process frustrating and time consuming. They usually have to stand over their young children and coach them through the entire chore. The effort expended in such supervising is often greater than the effort of cleaning up without the children's help.

Although straightening up after young children remains an adult task, there are ways you can involve your child. Your 2½- or 3-year-old can put a few toys back in place, particularly if you do the job with her or if you hand her the toys and tell her where they go. Your 4- or 5-year-old can take a more active role in straightening up, although she will still be most successful when you are close-by helping.

Your child may be willing to cooperate in cleanups if you give her some warning: "In five minutes it will be time to put the toys away." If your child seems overwhelmed by cleaning up, help her focus by giving specific instructions: "Jesse, you're in charge of putting the records and books away." Sometimes your child will go along with you if you offer concrete choices: "You can either put the trucks back on the shelf or put the toy figures in this basket." And when several children are playing together you can ask, "Who is going to put the crayons away? Who will clean up the train set?"

If you and your spouse work outside the home, you may want to strike a balance between your child's desire to play freely when she is home and your desire to keep cleanup to a minimum. Some evenings let her play with her toys in any way she wants, and on other evenings, structure her play so that she takes out only a few things such as crayons or a puzzle for use in a specific place.

If your children resist putting their toys away, there are many other household jobs they may be willing and able to do. These jobs can include dusting, washing windows and storm doors, vacuuming, putting silverware away, polishing silver, sweeping, and folding clothes. As they get older, your children will take on more responsibility for putting their things away and your job will become easier. In the meantime, your young children may occasionally surprise you with an unexpected cleanup, done just to help you out and make you happy.

CHILDREN'S THINKING

What Does My Child Think About Nature?

A young child's thoughts about the world are not based on logic and fact. When a child under 5 is asked about the sun, he may explain that a man lit a match and threw it up in the sky, and that's how the sun got there. Young children often believe that humans created the oceans, trees, space, mountains, and other natural phenomena. A child will ask, "Why did they make that mountain so high? Why did they put Switzerland so far away?" After a snowstorm, one child said, "I guess the people ran out of snowflakes."

Young children assume that inanimate objects have the same motives, intentions, and feelings a child has. One boy looked in his bucket after a downpour and said, "Guess what the rain did. It gave me water. Wasn't that nice?" Another child, trying his bike for the first time in several months, declared, "Look, my bike got smaller!" Sometimes a child will blame an object for a mishap: "That chair bumped into me!" And when a child misses a ball during a game of catch, he may not feel bad about his own abilities but may instead blame the ball: "That ball started flying crooked."

To a young child, many objects are alive. A pencil is alive because it writes, a cloud because it moves. Picture books and fairy tales entrance a child because they mirror his world by presenting talking objects and animals, and trees that walk and sing.

To find out what your child thinks about nature and the objects around him, listen to his explanations of events and ask, "How do you think the stars got there? Why do you think worms crawl?" When he asks you a question, ask for his thoughts first before you answer. You'll be delighted with your child's responses and fascinated by the insights you get into his thinking. Keep asking and notice the changing answers he gives as he grows older.

You may be tempted to correct your child when he gives you answers that are clearly not factual. Sometimes it is best to just accept what he says, although at other times you will want to offer as much information as you think he can understand. But don't be surprised if he listens and then sticks to his own thoughts and beliefs. This is natural behavior for children under 5 or 6 years old, who generally prefer their own ideas about the world.

My Child Asks Questions and Talks All the Time

Young children are natural learners and great observers of the here-and-now. They constantly try to gather information about what goes on around them, and that means they ask many questions and talk a lot. "Who's that?" "Why is she doing that?" "Where is that truck going?" Since a child believes that adults know everything, the child assumes that her parents will have the answer to each question. She also assumes that everything has a purpose that can be discovered just by asking. "Why is that man so tall?"

Sometimes a child uses questions to relieve her anxieties. She may ask, "Why is that dog barking?" because she is afraid of the animal. At other times a child might ask a stream of questions or talk on and on just to be sociable and to stay in constant contact with her parents.

Many times, as soon as parents have answered their child's question, the child asks the same question again, or follows her parents' explanation with an immediate, "Why?" This can be annoying because parents feel they are constantly replying to their child. At times it's hard to know what the child wants, since she is often not satisfied by the explanations she receives. If parents question their child before they offer a complex answer, they may gain some insight into the child's real needs. "What do you think that word means?" "Tell me why you think that man was running?"

Sometimes a child repeatedly asks "why" and rejects an answer because she doesn't understand it. She may have difficulty absorbing facts that aren't familiar or that don't relate directly to her experience. That's why parents should answer questions on a level that is appropriate for their child. And parents should expect to hear the same questions over and over because it takes time and repetition before a child masters complex information.

A child may occasionally ask a question that is difficult to answer. One 4-year-old from a family with three children asked her friend's mother, "Why do you only have two kids?" The mother, concerned that the child might be upset by an honest answer (two was all she wanted), put the question back to the child. "Why do you think I only have two children?" The child replied, "Because you wanted to," and was satisfied.

A problem often arises when young children ask socially embarrassing questions. You may be in a store with your child when she points to someone and loudly asks, "Why is he so fat?" Your child has no understanding of the man's feelings and asks only because she is spontaneous and curious. Yet you will naturally feel ashamed and sorry. The best you can do at such moments is give your child a brief, quiet answer ("That's just the way he looks") and then try to distract her or promise to discuss the situation later in private.

When your child's constant questions and general chatter bother you, remember that you don't have to be ready to respond at all times. You can acknowledge your child's talk by nodding or saying, "I'm listening," or even "Um hmm." Your child will know you are aware of her words and often that will be enough to make her happy.

Does My Child Know
What's Real and What's Not?

Young children often believe that whatever they hear and see is real. Until a child is 5 or 6 years old, his experience is limited and his ability to reason is not fully developed; therefore he can't always be "logical." It may not make sense to an adult, but to a young child clowns are real, everything on TV is true, everything other children say is true, and a disguise changes a person. The young child's inability to distinguish make-believe from reality explains his fear of monsters, masks, and costumed figures.

When a young child watches television, he thinks he is watching real life. One 4-year-old saw a Superman program followed by a televised demonstration intended to prove that Superman really didn't fly. A man lay down on a table and showed how camera tricks simulate flying. After the demonstration, the child's mother asked if the child still thought Superman could fly. "Yes," he answered, "but that man on the table couldn't."

It is very difficult to convince a child that television does not always represent the truth. The toys in commercials look magical and exciting as they talk and move around on their own. It takes years for a child to develop some skepticism about these advertisements. One young boy insisted that sugared cereal was good for him because television had told him so. His mother explained the purpose of commercials, but the child still believed what he had heard. Although parents usually can't change their young child's thinking, they can let him know their own opinions. "I know the cereal on TV looks good, but I think it's too sweet for breakfast." "TV makes it look as though Superman is flying, but I don't believe that he can really fly."

Just as a child believes what he hears on television, he also believes what other people, including young children, say to him. If a child's friend says, "There are bugs under your rug," or "The moon is a dead planet," or, in a moment of anger, "You're not coming to my party," the listener accepts the statement as truth, without questioning the other child's knowledge or motives.

Words are taken literally and have tremendous power. That's why a young child gets so upset when he is called "a dummy"; he feels he must shout back, "No, I'm not," or get someone else to reassure him. Children, especially those under 3, usually can't separate names from objects and people. A mother told her son that he was handsome and he said, "No, I'm not. I'm Jimmy." It takes time for children to realize that names are not parts of things, but are separate and often changeable.

Children can be confused not just by what they hear and see, but by what they imagine and dream. Children are not sure what dreams are or where they come from: do they come from the sky? from the bed? from the toys the child sleeps with? through the window? Frightening dreams seem very real to a child and vivid dreams seem part of real life. One child, who had dreamed that an airplane landed in the park behind his house, woke up believing the plane was really there. When his father tried to convince him otherwise, the child refused to listen. The father finally took his son to the park to show that there was no plane.

You can find out what your child thinks by questioning him, listening to him, and observing him. You will find that his thinking is different from adults' and that he believes many things that are not true. As long as he bases his thinking on appearances and his own experience, you may not be able to change his mind on many issues, but as he nears elementary school age, his logical understanding of the world will increase.

Why Isn't My Child
More Reasonable?

A father handed his daughter and her friend cups containing equal amounts of raisins. The daughter looked at both cups and said, "Alison has more. I want more." "But I gave you each the same amount," her father protested. The girl refused to accept the facts and continued to argue for more raisins.

Struggles often develop over such issues when children are 4 years old and under. These children base their reasoning on how things look, not necessarily on how things really are. If something appears right to a child, she will accept it, even if her acceptance defies logic. One child wanted a whole cup of juice, but her mother only had half a cup left. The child fussed and refused the drink until her mother poured it into a tiny cup. The small amount of juice filled the little cup and the child was happy, even though she still had the same amount of juice she had just refused as inadequate.

Parents can become frustrated when their children don't think logically. A parent can count out jelly beans to prove that all the children at a party have the same number, but the children often will not believe the shares are equal unless they "look" equal. A spread out pile may seem bigger than a compact one; a tall, thin container may appear to hold more than a short, wide one. Parents can demonstrate this pre-logical thinking with a simple experiment: they can line up peanuts in two identical rows, then spread one of the rows out. A child under 5 will say that the wider row now has more peanuts in it, even though the child saw that no new peanuts were added.

It is difficult, if not impossible, to change a young child's reasoning before she is developmentally ready to think logically. Once you realize that your child thinks differently than you do, you can understand why she so often rejects what seems perfectly reasonable. By the time she is 5 or 6, you will see dramatic changes in her thinking and reasoning abilities. Until then, you might want to accommodate her at times, rather than struggle to change her mind. One father, whose child wanted more ketchup even though she clearly had an adequate amount on her plate, simply spread his daughter's ketchup so it looked like a larger amount. The father avoided an argument, and the child was completely satisfied.

My Child Doesn't Think About Other People's Feelings

A 3½-year-old interrupted his mother's phone call: "Can I go outside?" His mother motioned for him to wait a minute, but he persisted. "Mom, Josh is outside. Can I ride my bike?" When she whispered for him to be quiet until she was off the phone, he walked away, but was back almost immediately: "Now can I go?" After the mother hung up, she felt frustrated with the interruptions and wondered why her son couldn't be more considerate and patient.

Most children under the age of 5 or 6 have a difficult time thinking of other people's feelings. Young children, as researcher Jean Piaget pointed out, are egocentric; they focus on their own immediate needs and interests, and consider only one side of any situation—their own. They don't do this to be selfish, although that is often the result. Children are generally incapable, during their early years, of putting themselves in another person's place or imagining how other people think. Egocentrism is a normal, although difficult, part of child development.

Parents see egocentric thinking and behavior when children play. One child will grab another's toy, others will hit and call each other names, two children will discuss the faults of a third who stands next to them, etc. When young children play board games, they often cheat, not caring about their opponent's chances. One child, who drew an unfavorable card while playing a game, said, "I'm just not listening to this card."

Parents try to change their children's actions and teach their children to stick to rules: "Don't hit, you'll hurt him," "He was using that," "You should include her in your game." Yet children have limited control over their thinking, and often forget to (or just cannot) consider others.

Frequent struggles over a child's self-centered ways can be very frustrating for parents. They may wonder if their child is particularly unpleasant or if he acts selfish to "get at" them, and they may also wonder if they have set firm enough limits. Do other children act this way? When, for instance, a child does not let his mother rest ("Mom, look at my picture!") even when she is not feeling well, the mother may wonder if her child has any considerate feelings at all.

Although at times your child may act egocentric because you have not set sufficient limits, more often he will behave this way because he is not yet able to consider other people's needs. Your expectations for your child's behavior should take into account this stage of development. If you always expect him to be polite and considerate, you and your child will find yourselves in constant conflict.

It is very important that you establish limits for your child and try to teach him appropriate behavior. But you should also try to be flexible and patient as your child grows through this stage and gradually learns to think about others' feelings and points of view. Of course, it is unrealistic to think you can always be understanding. You will often become angry at your child's thoughtless behavior, but understanding that this is a part of normal development is helpful. One mother became particularly upset and embarrassed as she heard her daughter tell a boy who could not come to her birthday party, "Oh, goody. Now we'll have enough chairs." Expect to hear such statements, but also be assured that eventually your child will learn to be more considerate.

I Want to Tell My Child
About Pregnancy and Birth

"Mom, how did the baby get in your stomach?" "How did I get born?" "Am I going to have a baby, too?" Parents are sometimes caught by surprise as their 3- to 5-year-old begins asking questions about sex and childbirth. Parents wonder how much to tell their child, and when to tell her. Some books and specialists advise parents to give young children all the facts about sex and reproduction, but children are often unable to absorb and comprehend such information. Learning about and understanding reproduction is a gradual process that continues through the childhood years.

Young children usually have their own ideas about how the human body works, based on their observations and experience. Before parents talk to their child about pregnancy, they should ask what she thinks. "How do you think the baby got inside of me?" Many children believe that eating too much causes pregnancy and that a woman gives birth in the same way she has a bowel movement. A child who has heard that a baby starts from a special seed might think that pregnancy comes from eating seeds. Parents may discover that their child is afraid of pregnancy, since children often fear things they don't understand and things they imagine. The child may believe, for instance, that she can get pregnant. By asking questions, parents find out about such thoughts and discover how to reassure their child.

Before you offer your 3- to 5-year-old child the facts about pregnancy and birth, wait for her to ask questions. There is no need to volunteer information if she is not yet curious about the subject. And when she does ask questions, don't overwhelm her with information. Start with simple explanations: "The baby grows in a special place inside the mother." Such a statement may satisfy her only for a few minutes or it may be enough for six months. Wait for your child to ask for more before you continue your discussion; don't feel that you have to tell all the facts at one time.

If you do explain too much too soon, your child may become confused or upset. One 4-year-old girl, after hearing the details of childbirth, declared, "I'm never going to have a baby." A 3½-year-old, who had been enrolled in a sibling childbirth class where he heard all the facts about birth, still believed "Mom's stomach unzips so the baby can get out." Both these children were too young to handle the information as it was given to them. If your child seems curious about pregnancy and birth, explain the facts in simple terms that she can understand. You will satisfy her curiosity without overwhelming her. Then, when she is older she will have an easier time understanding, cognitively and emotionally, the facts of pregnancy.

FEARS AND IMAGINATION

Out of Sight, Out of Mind

Until a child is 8 or 9 months old, he believes that objects and people exist only if he can see them. If you take a toy away from your child and hide it behind your back as he watches, he will act as though there no longer is a toy. In the same way, when you leave your child's side to go into another room, he may believe you no longer exist. Your disappearance frightens your infant, which explains the anxiety and tears you see when you leave his sight.

When you play peek-a-boo with your baby, you re-enact the anxiety and relief he feels each time you leave and return. You hide behind your hands or a scarf and your baby believes you are no longer there. He may even become momentarily upset and whimper. When you suddenly reappear and say peek-a-boo, he laughs with delight to have you back.

By 9 or 10 months, a child begins to have some idea that objects exist even when he can't see them. At this age he may look for a hidden toy if he saw you put it behind your back or under a pillow. But at times your baby may still react with fear and uncertainty when you leave him because his understanding of people's permanence is not fully developed and won't be until he is 2 or 3 years old.

My Child Is Afraid
to Have a Haircut

It is hard to give a haircut to children under 2 because they wriggle around so much, and it is hard to cut the hair of children over 2 because they are often afraid of haircuts, and struggle and resist. Two- and 3-year-olds have a general fear of bodily harm, and often believe that haircuts hurt, that their hair won't grow back, that shampoo will get in their eyes and sting, and that they will be helpless sitting in front of a stranger with scissors.

You should talk to your child about getting a haircut, and reassure her that it is a painless procedure. She may feel less anxious if she has a doll to play barber with. As she washes and cuts (or pretends to cut) the doll's hair, she may begin to feel in control of a situation that frightens her.

If your child is very young, or quite frightened of haircuts, you may want to cut her hair at home. You or a relative or close friend can cut her hair as she sits in her high chair and plays with some of her toys or watches you in a mirror. Since it is hard for young children to hold still, and since you are probably not an experienced stylist, you shouldn't expect your child's home haircut to be perfect.

When your child is 3 or 4, she may be willing to visit a professional stylist. For a first haircut, go to someone recommended by other parents or someone who specializes in cutting children's hair. Before you bring your child in for an appointment, you might want to observe the stylist—does he or she seem gentle? patient?—and talk to him or her about your child's anxiety.

Your child might feel comfortable going to the same barber shop or beauty shop you use. She may have seen your stylist at work already and be familiar with the surroundings and the people in the shop. Taking your child with you when you (or your older child, if you have one) get a haircut is a good way to help her get over her fears. If your child resists professional haircuts but you are determined to take her to a stylist, try to distract her by giving her a few plastic rollers to hold or a lollypop to eat while she is in the chair, or by promising her a treat. One mother held her son on her lap during haircuts when he was under 2, and when he was over 2, she held his hand and tried to distract him with a few play things.

When your child is 4 or 5, she may stop being afraid of haircuts but may develop anxieties about hairstyles. She may have a clear preference for a particular look: long hair, short hair, bangs, a ponytail. One boy told his mother he wanted a curl on his forehead "just like Superman's." If you don't agree with your child's choice, the two of you may struggle before each haircut. Try to remember your own childhood arguments about hair, and how it felt to have no control over your looks. If you let your child know you respect her choices, and if you compromise whenever possible ("You can wear a barrette this afternoon," "During the winter you can let your hair grow"), trips to the hair cutters will usually go smoothly.

Should I Prepare Him for Doctor Appointments?

Many children have negative feelings—based on past experience and fearful imaginings—about seeing a doctor. If a child is under 2 years old, his parents will have a difficult time preparing him for an appointment. A child this young, who will not fully understand the reasons for his visit, may enter the doctor's office calmly and then cry or feel anxious when he goes into the examining room. Many parts of a standard check-up are uncomfortable: the child gags as his throat is checked, he feels momentary pain during blood tests and inoculations, he is measured and tested with cold instruments. No matter how well mannered the physician is, the examination can be an unpleasant and therefore fearful experience for a very young child.

During an examination, the parents of a child under 2 can try to offer comfort and reassurance: "I'm right here beside you," "I know you don't like to have your ears checked," "The doctor is almost done." But such words won't usually relieve the child's anxiety, especially when, as often happens, his parents are physically restraining him so the doctor can continue the examination. Sometimes a child in this situation will feel comforted if his pacifier, bottle, or blanket is nearby.

Parents are often more successful helping a child between 3 and 5 years old deal with a fear of doctors. A child at this stage is better able to understand what happens during an examination and to verbalize some of his anxieties. If you are taking a child this age to the doctor, talk to your child ahead of time about the appointment. Tell him briefly about the procedures, the instruments the doctor will use, the toys in the waiting room, the set-up of the examining rooms, etc., but try to present this information in a way that will not frighten your child: "Do you remember the table in the examining room? I can read you a story while you sit up there and wait for the doctor." "There are cups in the examining room so you can get a drink of water there." If an injection is scheduled, let your child know: "Your shot might hurt, but only for a moment."

If your child is afraid of doctors, you might be tempted to keep the appointment from him; you may even consider starting out for the office without letting your child know where you both are going. Although this may seem like a good way to keep your child from getting upset, deceiving him is actually a mistake. You deprive him of time to prepare for the visit, and you may increase his fear. He might believe that you didn't tell him about the appointment because there was something to be afraid of. It is always better to let your child know in advance about an office visit.

To find out what your child's specific fears are, ask, "What do you think the doctor will do?" When your child expresses his fears, accept them; don't pressure him to "be brave" or "be good." When a child knows that he can say "ouch" or cry, he actually feels less upset about getting an injection or having his ears and throat checked.

Your child may tell you he is anxious about taking his clothes off in the doctor's office. This is a common worry for children 4 to 5 years old. Let your child know he may have to undress, but then talk to your doctor about the situation. Many pediatricians will accommodate a modest child by weighing or examining him while he is partly clothed.

Your child may relieve some of his own anxiety about appointments by playing doctor. When your child takes the role of doctor, he is in control as he re-experiences some of the uncomfortable and frightening things that have happened to him. Children usually play doctor by giving pretend injections and using bandages, but occasionally they undress and examine each other. You may be uncomfortable with such play, but there is no need to worry. This is a common, innocent occurrence, and you should try not to make your child feel ashamed for playing this way. Just gently set limits.

No matter how well you prepare your child for his doctor visit, he may remain anxious and afraid. Some children are just more worried than others about appointments and doctors. As long as your child is fearful, the best you can do is accept your child's feelings, give him honest information about what to expect, and offer him reassurance.

What Should I Tell My Child About the Dentist?

The mouth is a source of pleasure for a young child. As an infant, he sucked from the breast or bottle, and later discovered how enjoyable food was. He may have sucked on his thumb or a pacifier, and he learned about toys and other objects by putting them in his mouth. When a young child feels discomfort or pain in his mouth (from teething, sore gums, etc.) the experience can seem intolerable to him. And he may strongly resist a visit to the dentist, even though he will only feel mildly uncomfortable there.

Most children first go for a dental check-up when they are 3 or 3½ years old. A younger child will go if he has a problem with his teeth or gums. Although a child under 3 will probably not understand what a dental visit is about, his parents should still try to prepare him by describing, in a simple way, the dentist's procedures: "The dentist is going to look inside your mouth and check your teeth and I'll be there with you." At the office, a very young child might cooperate if he is examined while sitting on his parent's lap. If this is not possible, his parents should at least stay nearby to offer reassurance and comfort.

A child who is 3 or older is usually able to cooperate and follow directions well enough to be examined by a dentist. When your child is going for his first check-up, you should talk to him about who the dentist is and what he or she will be looking for. Try acting out a visit to the office. Your child may overcome some of his fears if he can take an active role playing the dentist. You can help prepare your child for his dental appointment by reading him picture books on the subject and you can call the dentist's office before the appointment and ask for advice on how to help your child feel less anxious about the examination.

Despite your preparations, your child may still enter the dentist's office feeling fearful, and what he sees and hears there may make him feel worse. The sound of the drill can be frightening, and the dentist's instruments look sharp. When a child is sitting down in the chair, he can feel vulnerable and afraid since he does not have control over what goes into his mouth. Encourage your child to express his feelings and to ask the dentist questions: "Will that hurt me? When will you be done?" If you have chosen a dentist who is sensitive and likes children, he or she will be happy to reassure your child and explain the procedures, perhaps providing a mirror so your child can watch. You or the dentist might be able to distract your child by talking about the "treasure" he will take home after the appointment.

It sometimes happens that parents are more afraid of dental examinations than their children are. If you are apprehensive about dentists, try not to pass your anxieties on to your child, who may be surprisingly willing to go for a check-up.

My Child Has
an Imaginary Friend

Many parents worry when their children, usually between the ages of 3 and 4, create imaginary friends. Parents wonder, "Why does he need one? Can't he tell the difference between a real person and a pretend one?" And while parents are sometimes amused by their child's concerns ("Watch out! You'll sit on Herman!"), they are more often frustrated.

Yet an imaginary friend is an important and creative part of growing up for many children. The friend helps a child deal with emotions and problems that the child might otherwise not be able to handle. For example, a child might invent a companion as a way of relieving loneliness when he moves to a new home, leaving his real friends behind. Or the imaginary friend might help the child deal with a new baby in the family, the start of day care or nursery school, or tension at home. Sometimes a child creates an imaginary animal, such as a dog, to help overcome a fear of real dogs.

If a child feels overly controlled or unaccepted by his parents, he may invent a companion who is very accepting and who always likes him. The child may even become a demanding "parent" to his friend, whom he imagines to be a powerless child: "Herman, that was very bad. You shouldn't have done that."

Sometimes a child will use an imaginary companion to relieve himself of guilt. Since a child who has done something wrong fears discipline and the loss of his parents' love, he may deny his misbehavior ("I didn't do it") even when he has been caught. If he greatly fears rejection, he may blame his imaginary friend for his own misdeeds. That way he will not have to deal with criticism, responsibility, or bad feelings about himself: "Herman took the papers off your desk," or "Herman made me do it." In such a situation, parents can say, "I can't allow you or Herman to play with my papers," or "You messed up the papers on my desk and I want you to help me clean them up."

If your child has an imaginary friend, you may wonder what to do about the situation. Should you set an extra place at the table, as your child requests, or will your acceptance of the

companion just prolong the fantasy? Compromise is the best solution. It is certainly all right to go along with some of your child's requests for his imaginary friend. And as long as you are patient with your child, it is also all right to set limits: "You may talk about your friend, but we are not going to change our routine for him right now." If you are worried because your child believes in an imaginary character, keep in mind that we encourage children to believe in the tooth fairy, Santa Claus, and other pretend characters. The main difference between these and your child's friend is that the friend is your child's own creation.

If you think your child is involved in fantasy because he feels powerless, consider the amount of freedom you allow him. You may want to give him more opportunities to express his feelings and to explore. And if your child seems lonely because of a recent move or the lack of nearby playmates, help him to find real friends who can eventually take the place of the imaginary one.

As your child grows and becomes better able to handle criticism, he will give up his pretend companion. Your child will gradually take on the qualities and responsibilities he assigned to his friend, and may come to recognize that the friend was actually part of himself.

Halloween Is Difficult
for My Child

Young children regard Halloween with a mixture of excitement and uneasiness. On one hand, the holiday means candy, dressing up, and a full day of fun with friends; but on the other hand, it means strange sights, frightening sounds, and darkness. The ambivalence that children feel about the two sides of Halloween carries over to most aspects of the holiday, including anticipation, picking out costumes, and trick-or-treating. And parents have ambivalent feelings too, about the issues of safety and eating sweets.

Before Halloween begins, some parents find that their child's behavior changes. She may become more silly or aggressive, or may whine more than usual, asking again and again, "When will Halloween begin?" Much of the difficulty before the holiday centers around the child's desire to wear her costume. If she is allowed to dress up in it before Halloween, she may have an easier time waiting for the enjoyable as well as the scary activities to begin. She may also feel less anxious if she can mark off the remaining days on a calendar or tear one piece of a paper chain off for each day left before October 31.

Some parents, as part of the pre-Halloween excitement, buy or borrow holiday books. Yet Halloween books often have pictures and ideas that can frighten young children, who believe that what they see in a book is real. If a Halloween story is too frightening, parents can change the words as they read, or try creating their own family Halloween picture books.

The most exciting part of Halloween is usually picking out and wearing a costume. Children enjoy dressing up because they can experiment with fantasy and try out different roles: they can be television characters or superheroes or grownup workers. Children often change their minds about which costume to wear, and sometimes argue with their parents about costume choices. In most cases, parents should let their child choose her own disguise.

Some children are afraid of costumes, especially costumes designed to be frightening. Since young children do not fully understand the difference between reality and make-believe, they are not convinced that a scary ghost or a monster is only pretend. Even when they know the person under the disguise, they may respond to the costume with fear.

Because of their fears, some young children don't want to dress up for Halloween. This can make parents feel uneasy or embarrassed as they wonder why their child doesn't like Halloween when other children seem to. Parents in this situation should try to remember that all children are different—ones with older siblings may feel more comfortable in costumes, and outgoing children may enjoy dressing up more than reserved children do. The age of a child makes a big difference, and older children, who are better able to understand that a real person is behind each mask, enjoy holiday costumes more.

If your child is afraid of costumes, you should try to reassure her while letting her know that you understand her fears. You can say, "Costumes look scary, but they're only pretend. People pretend to be ghosts just as you dress up to pretend you're a fire fighter." Sometimes such statements work, but often they don't. If your child is afraid, and you've tried unsuccessfully to lessen her worries, don't pressure her. Eventually she will grow out of her fears.

Sometimes a child will wear a costume but not a mask. Masks

partially cover a child's eyes and face, and this may intensify her fears. Try using face make-up instead of a mask, or help your child make a mask that she can hold up to her face rather than wear. Such a mask will let her exert quick control, and may make her feel more comfortable.

When Halloween night comes, and most children's costumes are on, the trick-or-treating begins. Your child may find this to be a difficult part of the holiday. It's dark and there are many people outside, all looking like strangers, many looking very spooky. A child who finds costumes frightening may be overwhelmed by the sight of so many disguised trick-or-treaters.

Your child may be afraid to go to trick-or-treating at other people's homes. All year long you have told her not to talk to strangers or go to unfamiliar houses, yet on Halloween night it is suddenly acceptable to go and ask for candy. A neighbor's house may seem strange if your child has never played inside. And your child may be afraid either that people will answer their doors wearing scary costumes or that she will have to stand at a doorstep with other children dressed in frightening disguises.

Your 2- or 3-year-old may hesitate to trick-or-treat because she has never done it before. And if your child is shy, she may not want to talk to neighbors, even if you stand in the background reassuring or coaching her: "Now say trick-or-treat." Many children don't like to be focused on, even by people who admire their costumes: "Oh, look at the cute bunny! Who's under there?"

There's another side to trick-or-treat anxiety: your concerns about your child's safety. Because of frightening news stories, many parents warn their children about unwrapped candy, spend time looking through their children's bags for open or suspicious food, and even take their children to hospitals to have candy X-rayed. Schools reinforce the need for safety with lectures and programs on holiday danger. All of this may be necessary, but it also tends to make children feel frightened and unsure about the holiday. In order to avoid the possibility of unsafe food, some parents decide to skip trick-or-treating altogether, instead trying community parties, costume parades, home parties, or Halloween craft treats.

If you do allow trick-or-treating, you will have another Halloween problem: what to do with all the candy. Some parents let their children eat one or two pieces on Halloween night; other parents let them eat whatever they want. The days following the holiday can be difficult if your child doesn't lose interest in her candy. If you choose eventually to throw the goodies out, let your child know ahead of time so that she can pick out a few special pieces to save, and explain that you are getting rid of the candy because it's unhealthy to eat too many sweets. If your child protests strongly, wait a day or so and then discuss the issue again. Through all of this it might help you to realize that, while Halloween can be an exciting time, it's not always easy for the families of young children.

What Can I Do About
My Child's Fear of Monsters?

All children have bedtime fears: they worry about a monster in the closet, an alligator under the bed, or a skeleton at the window. Such frightening images are part of a child's internal world. At night, when the stimulations and distractions of the day are over, a child may begin to focus on this world and on the anxious thoughts and feelings that were stirred up during the day. Worries about a new school, a move, or parents' arguments can cause a child to feel afraid. And bedtime darkness makes the child feel even more scared and vulnerable.

Fears of monsters, witches, and other bad things sometimes originate with a child's own anger. Adults seldom remember the intensity of childhood emotions. Anger is often rage: the determination to have, to control, and to do for themselves is very strong in children. And because they are egocentric, children assume that adults feel the same things they do. A child who is angry enough to hurt someone or destroy something may believe that the powerful adults around him, like monsters, feel angry enough to hurt him. This is a scary proposition.

Because a child isn't comfortable with hostile thoughts aimed at his parents, he unconsciously projects his own feelings onto them or onto monsters. Instead of thinking, "I'm so angry at Mom and Dad," he thinks, "Mom and Dad are so angry at me." The result of this projection can be an increased fear of monsters and other frightening creatures.

The specific scary images that frighten a child can be introduced by a television show, a movie, a fairy tale, or even a picture in a book. Some parents who try to alleviate a child's fears by showing him a book about nice monsters may actually be giving him something else to be afraid of. This can happen because the young child has difficulty distinguishing what is real from what is not. Once he sees a picture of a monster, even a harmless one, he may be convinced that such a thing exists. Therefore, parents may want to keep a sensitive child from seeing scary books, television shows, or movies.

If your child tells you he is frightened of monsters, try to reassure him. For example, you can say, "Sometimes children think that monsters are real, but I don't believe there are such things. You are very safe here." Be careful not to pressure your child into agreeing that his fears are irrational. And don't dismiss his fears by saying, "Don't be afraid." Children who are told their fears are silly will continue to feel afraid but may not openly express themselves because they anticipate being ridiculed or ashamed. Instead, they may cry, cling, or have frequent scary dreams.

Try to get your child to express his fears, since talking about them can help him deal with them. The inability to discuss fears can make them feel more real and give them more power. You might ask your child, "What does a monster do? What does it look like? Can you draw a picture of it? Where did you think you saw it?" Such questions will help you learn more about what frightens your child. When your child is frightened you may have to spend more time than usual sitting with him, reassuring him at bedtime. You may feel more patient about this if you remember your own childhood fears. Although you received assurances from your parents, you still believed that frightening things lurked in the closets and under the bed.

No matter how long you sit with your child, talk with him, or comfort him, he will not give up his fears easily. You can help him best by reassuring him about his safety and acknowledging his fears while letting him know that one day he will be able to master them.

Why Is My Child Afraid
of Santa Claus?

A beautifully dressed 2-year-old waits in line to see Santa Claus. When it's her turn, Santa says, "Come here, little girl," and the girl's parents say, "Go sit on his lap." The child listens, looks at the smiling face in front of her, and bursts into tears. This child is afraid of Santa.

It surprises people to learn that many children fear such a friendly character. After all, from a parent's perspective Santa represents love and the spirit of gift giving. When a child resists sitting on kind Santa's lap, her parents become embarrassed and easily wonder, "What's wrong with my child?" Parents may try to force their child onto Santa or use threats and bribes: "If you sit on Santa's lap you'll get a lot of toys for Christmas." Even when parents are patient they are usually unsuccessful in getting their child to come in contact with Santa. Young children struggle and resist Santa out of fear, and it's almost impossible to convince a scared child not to be afraid.

Most children under the age of 5 believe that what they hear and see is real. They regard their own perspective as absolute and for them, Santa is real. Children see him in shopping malls, they read and sing about him, and their parents talk as though he truly existed.

This Santa, with a rather deep voice and a beard that covers most of his face, can be scary looking and unpleasant to a young child. Since the child is in contact with Santa only during the

Christmas season, he is unfamiliar and children do not go to unfamiliar people with ease. The child is not sure he's nice and her parents aren't always reassuring about his looks. While they tell her that a Halloween character or a clown is only someone dressed in a costume, they don't say that Santa, too, is wearing a costume. They don't want her to know.

A young child's belief in a real Santa can take on a mysterious quality, giving Santa tremendous power. Santa "knows" when the child is good or bad, and he decides which gifts she will receive. He seems omnipotent, flying through the sky, entering the child's home when she is asleep, watching her all the time. It can be frightening for her to think about Santa coming at night and when she learns that he arrives through the chimney she begins to wonder, "How will he fit? What if he falls? How does he get the toys down the chimney?" If there is no chimney, "How will he get in?"

A child may worry about being judged by Santa, who will decide if she has been good enough to receive gifts on Christmas. And her parents, not realizing she is already under a lot of pressure during this time of the year, may say, "You'd better be good or Santa won't bring you a present." Adults often use this line when they are frustrated with children's behavior, but it adds a threatening note to the fun and excitement of Christmas gift giving. A child who hears this threat repeatedly may become anxious, silly, aggressive, or fearful.

Realistically, a child cannot live up to Santa's or her parents' expectations of good behavior. Young children struggle when they have to pick up their toys, they do not like to go to bed, they usually do not brush their teeth or wash their hands and faces without being reminded (at least twice), and they usually don't help with day-to-day chores. It's not that children are "bad," it's that parents' and Santa's expectations are unrealistic.

Given Santa's power to judge, his unusual appearance, and his ability to see and be everywhere, it is not surprising when a young child has very ambivalent feelings about approaching him. She wants to tell him what to bring for Christmas and she wants to please her parents, but she is afraid.

Fortunately, if your child fears Santa, there are a variety of things you can do ahead of time to help her feel better. The most important is to reassure and prepare her by talking about Santa, mentioning his size, voice, and clothes. You can explain that Santa is friendly and enjoys talking with children about Christmas. You can also try letting your child go up to Santa with a sibling or friend. Be selective about the Santas you visit, asking your friends about their experiences at various shopping centers, and watching a Santa to see how he acts with young children. A Santa who doesn't put too much pressure on children will make you and your child more comfortable.

Finally, consider your child's age and personality when deciding how far to go during the Santa visit. A shy child might display more apprehension than an out-going child. A 2- or 3-year-old will be more frightened than a 4- or 5-year-old. And children with confident older siblings can often be convinced that Santa is nice and likes children.

Whatever you try, your child may still cry and refuse to go to Santa. If this happens, step back with her and try to find a good alternative activity such as waving to Santa or sitting down to watch. In a year or so there are bound to be changes in your child's attitudes, and even though she cries this year, she may have fun visiting Santa next Christmas.

TOYS, PLAY, AND SOCIALIZING

Which Toys Are Appropriate?

Play is an essential part of growing up. While a child plays freely, he satisfies his curiosity and finds out how to use objects; he learns to plan and classify; he begins to evaluate, predict, question, discover, draw conclusions, and solve problems; and he also learns how to interact with his peers and imitate the people around him. A child whose play is not disturbed by adults' negative judgments ("The colors in that painting should really be blue and green," "If you pile any more blocks up, your building will fall") gains confidence through play, and rarely has a fear of failure.

Some parents minimize the importance of play, looking instead for "educational" activities for their child. But a child doesn't need pre-packaged devices in order to learn. Parents best nurture their child's drive to learn by following up on his interests, giving him many opportunities to play, and providing appropriate toys and materials.

The following are suggestions for age-appropriate toys and activities for your child. The list is by no means complete, and the ages listed are quite flexible. One child will enjoy a toy at 18 months, while another child will not play with that toy until he is 3 years old. Some children return again and again to toys they used when they were younger. And a child with an older sibling will get an early introduction to toys intended for older children. As your child grows, he will let you know which toys interest him and which activities he wishes to pursue.

Birth to 6 Months

An infant likes to look at objects around him; by 3 to 4 months he may be accidentally batting toys with his hands or feet, and by 4 to 6 months he may intentionally try to touch and grasp objects. During the earliest months you can hang mobiles from the crib or ceiling, put a safe mirror against the side of the crib, or secure a colorful pinwheel to the hood of the baby carriage. Once your child grasps objects, you can provide soft toys that can safely go in his mouth and that will not harm him if he bumps against them: a rattle or squeaking toy, teething beads, toys with faces.

6 to 12 Months

Once your baby can sit up, attach a busy box to the side of his crib. He will enjoy one with buttons, dials, pop-ups, and other things he can control. You can also give him kitchen items to play with such as pots and pans, plastic bowls and spoons, and a spillproof container filled with water that he can shake and watch. He will like cuddly dolls, squeeze toys, soft cars and trucks, large balls, hollow blocks made from heavy cardboard, and cloth or cardboard books. You can make books for your child by slipping pictures into a photo album.

12 to 18 Months

Your child will enjoy trucks or cars he can sit on, push-and-pull toys, doll carriages, plastic lawn mowers, wheelbarrows, a two-step kitchen stool he can stand on to see high places, pounding boards, toy telephones, music boxes, rocking horses, outside and indoor climbing equipment with ladders and slides, and adults' shoes he can walk around in. He will also like simple toys he can take apart, and plastic bottles with tops to take off and put on.

18 to 24 Months

Your child will enjoy stringing large wooden beads, screwing and unscrewing bottle caps, using a punching bag, pushing a toy shopping cart, using plastic tools, playing with balls of different sizes and shapes, arranging magnets on the refrigerator, and playing with stuffed animals. He may be happy for long periods playing with sand or water if he has shovels, pails, measuring cups, sieves, funnels, and plastic bottles to use. Although he will not be able to pedal yet, he may enjoy a Big Wheel or a small bike without pedals.

2 to 3 Years

A child this age may enjoy rubber, plastic, or wooden animals; dolls and dolls' accessories; a play stove, refrigerator, and sink with dishes, pots, and pans; dress-up clothes; a play house; a doctor's kit; large blocks; cars, trucks, a play fire house and fire engine, and a toy garage and gas station. Most 2- and 3-year-olds can use pens, paint, crayons, chalk (fun to use on the sidewalk), big paint brushes to use with water outside, and, when closely supervised, safety scissors. Your child will probably have fun jumping on a mattress that is flat on the floor, kicking a deflated ball that can't roll away from him, and riding a tricycle. He will also like using puzzles, playing musical instruments, and listening to records or tapes of folk, classical, children's music, etc.

4 to 5 Years

A child this age will like using arts and crafts materials such as pens, pencils, markers, scissors, tape, glue, string, play dough, clay, watercolors, tempera (which can be mixed with soap flakes to help prevent stains), and finger paints. Wagons, Big Wheels, and bikes with or without training wheels are fun as are balls, bats, frisbees, bubble blowers, kites, bowling pins, balance boards, old tires to swing or jump on, and bean bags to toss. Some of the most popular games for this age group are Candy Land, Hungry Hungry Hippos, Sorry, various matching games, Fish, and Old Maid. You can try offering your child practical things to play with, such as flashlights, magnifying glasses, whistles, simple tools, old household objects he can safely take apart, and banks; rakes and snow shovels; a funnel, pump, and eggbeater to use while playing with water and bubbles; and a large plastic needle for sewing burlap. Your child may enjoy building with Tinker Toys, Legos, and all kinds of blocks, and may want to make forts and houses out of blankets or large cardboard boxes. You can help your child make a puppet theatre from a table turned on its side; your child can run the show with play tickets, play money, and a toy cash register. A child this age is influenced by his friends and by TV and may want whatever toy other children have.

When you provide toys for a child of any age, avoid giving

too many that are pre-done or that limit creative play. So many toys can only be put together and used in one way, and if your child spends all his play time with such toys, he will have little chance to make his own creations. Instead look for toys that can be used in a variety of ways, and ones that allow your child

to use his imagination. For example, instead of buying kits of shrinkable plastic with pre-drawn pictures, buy the same plastic, without the drawings, at a craft store. Then your child can make his own designs.

As you buy toys for your child, you may find that he becomes intensely interested in a new plaything for several weeks, and then loses interest. This is common, although it may be disturbing to you if you have spent time and energy shopping for the right toy, one your child said he "wanted so badly." A child loses interest in toys for several reasons: he may have quickly exhausted all the toy's play possibilities, he may have mastered the toy, figuring out how it works, or he may be frustrated because the toy is not well made or is difficult to use.

To get more use from your child's discarded but almost new toys, put them away in a closet for several months. When you take them out, they will seem unfamiliar to your child, and he may become interested in them again. He may even think of new ways to play with the old toys, since his interests and ways of playing are always changing.

A Doll for My Son? A Truck for My Daughter?

There are toys that all children use—balls, puzzles, blocks, clay, crayons, board games—and there are "boy" toys and "girl" toys. Some parents try to avoid stereotyped or sexist toys and allow their children to choose playthings from the full range available. But other parents are uncomfortable when their children play with non-traditional toys. These parents, who do not buy cars and action figures for their girls or baby carriages and tea sets for their boys, fear that playing with toys intended for the opposite sex weakens a child's identification with his or her own sex.

Some parents may discourage their daughter when she acts like a "tomboy" or shows an interest in aggressive, supposedly masculine toys. But parents who pressure their child to follow traditionally feminine pursuits may seriously limit her potential.

Parents of boys can also restrict their child's development by demanding only masculine activities. Nursery school and day care teachers often hear parents tell their sons that the classroom's housekeeping area is "just for girls." Yet there is nothing wrong with a boy who wants to play house or dolls. Boys need to learn how to nurture, just as girls do, and an interest in playing house is perfectly normal.

Some parents, who don't mind if their children play with non-traditional toys, still feel uncomfortable buying such toys. One mother was pleased that her son played with dolls at his friend's house, but she couldn't bring herself to get him a doll when he asked. Similarly, a parent did not mind her daughter's using war toys in the neighborhood but resisted buying her a tank of her own.

Some parents who have children of both sexes encourage their sons and daughters to share toys, thus allowing non-traditional play. Other parents buy each sibling a few toys intended for the opposite sex so that brothers and sisters can play well together. One little girl had her own set of transforming robots to use whenever her brother's playmates came to the house. She joined in the boys' games and her parents avoided the struggles that come when one child is excluded. The girl's brother had a doll that he could use when his sister's friends visited.

When a child is under the age of 3 or 4 he or she will probably be attracted to toys of interest to both sexes, but by the time children are 5 they clearly identify which toys "belong" to which sex. One 5-year-old girl noticed a 2½-year-old boy wearing nail polish and she began to question him about his interests: "Do you like Barbie? Do you like robots?" When he answered yes to both questions she turned to her mom and said, "He's girlish-boyish."

Parents who encourage a child to play with whatever toys he or she likes—regardless of sex stereotypes—are often surprised when their child chooses the traditional "girl" or "boy" toys anyway. Girls are drawn to dolls, toy houses, and dressing up, while boys are attracted to cars, war toys, and space toys. Girls enjoy playing baby and house; boys like playing pirates, fire fighters, and guns. Certainly the media have a powerful influence here. Advertisers clearly market their toys for a particular sex and children never have a chance to see non-traditional play on commercials. But even considering the influence of television, children seem to have their own innate interests in typical, traditional play.

Given this strong drive girls have to play with "girl" toys, and boys have to play with "boy" toys, there is no need for parents to worry when their child shows an interest in toys for the opposite sex. And there is no reason parents should not buy non-traditional toys if their child wants them. Ultimately the child should choose what to play with.

In rare cases, parents might observe that their child seems abnormally dissatisfied with his or her gender. A child who consistently tries to play and act like a member of the opposite sex may be influenced by genetic factors, may sense his or her parents' disappointment ("I wish he'd been a girl!"), or may be reacting to family stress. Parents who are concerned about their child's behavior should seek professional guidance.

What About Homemade Toys?

Although stores offer a multitude of toys, you can create kits and playthings that provide enjoyment and encourage children to be creative. The following are suggestions for games, toys, and gifts for 2- to 5-year-olds. The kits take time to assemble, but probably no more time than searching the stores for the "right" toy. And your child will have fun helping you put these playthings together and decorating storage boxes with crayons or contact paper. Choose materials that are appropriate for your child's age, and supervise your child as he plays.

Art Box

In a plastic or cardboard shoe box, place any of the following supplies: colored pencils, magic markers, crayons, chalk, yarn, string, pipe cleaners, watercolor paints with brushes, small sheets of paper, glue, tape, tissue paper, felt, scraps of fabric, a ruler, old greeting cards, Popsicle sticks, strips of cardboard or balsa wood, scissors, and a hole puncher.

Play Office

In a large plastic or cardboard file box place any of the following: a stapler, a clipboard, a looseleaf binder with paper, stationery, folders, pencils and pens, envelopes, paper clips, an eraser, stickers, stamps and a stamp pad, and rubber bands.

Tool Box

Make a kit including: a hammer (plastic for 2-year-olds), nails, a screwdriver, a wrench, pliers, nuts and bolts, measuring tape, sandpaper, a child's saw, and styrofoam pieces to put nails and screws in. Wood scraps can often be found for free at lumber yards. You can drive nails and screws partway into a piece of wood 12″ × 6″. Then a young child can hammer and unscrew on these safely. Children should be supervised by an adult when they use the tool box.

Play Dough

To make your own play dough, use the following ingredients: 1 cup of flour; ½ cup of salt; 2 teaspoons of cream of tartar; 1 cup of water; 2 tablespoons of oil; 1 tablespoon of food coloring (optional). Combine the first three ingredients in a large saucepan. Gradually stir in the water mixed with the oil and food coloring. Cook over medium heat, stirring constantly until a ball forms. Remove the dough from the heat and knead it until it is smooth. The dough can be stored in plastic bags or containers, and put in a kit with cookie cutters, a rolling pin, small cups, an empty egg carton, empty thread spools, plastic knives, or other objects that would be fun to use with dough.

Sewing Kit

In a cardboard box or a lunchbox, place: cardboard, poster board, large plain file cards, a hole puncher, string, a plastic needlepoint needle, yarn, burlap, and scissors.

Forest Ranger or Camper Kit

In a knapsack or cardboard box, store: a canteen, a flashlight, a compass, nature books, binoculars, a whistle, sticks, a magnifying glass, a hat, and boots.

Beautician's Supplies

In a large plastic bag or box put: a mirror, curlers, hair pins, a blow-dryer (toy or real with the cord cut off), combs, brushes, towels, magazines, empty plastic shampoo bottles, emery boards, play makeup, jewelry, a pencil, paper, and play money.

Painter's Kit

You can use a bucket to store: a hat (which you may find for free at a paint supply store), different sized brushes, a paint roller, an old piece of sheet for a drop cloth, a rag, and sandpaper. Your child can paint outdoors with water.

Fire Fighter's Equipment

This kit, which can be stored in a big cardboard box, can include: a fire hat, raincoat, boots, an old cut piece of garden hose, a pretend walkie-talkie, goggles, and gloves.

Doctor's Kit

In a box or bag, place: cotton balls, a play thermometer, empty pill bottles, labels, paper, pens, an old white shirt, bandages, plastic syringes, and a toy stethoscope. Some of these supplies may be obtained for free from your pediatrician.

Sets like these can also be made for police officers, scientists, nurses, shoe salespersons, grocers, astronauts, magicians, and waiters/waitresses. You can vary the contents of these kits as your child grows and changes. If you decide to give one of these homemade toys as a gift, let your child help with the wrapping. She can color on white tissue paper or newsprint and make her own card by folding paper in half and decorating it.

Do Coloring Books
Limit Creativity?

There are many kinds of coloring books available: cartoon books, "educational" books, animal and history books, etc. They all are based on the same activity—a child colors a pre-drawn picture. Although this activity may seem enjoyable to an adult, a young child who spends too much time with coloring books may miss out on the chance to create his own artwork and know the enjoyment of drawing.

Parents sometimes buy coloring books because they think coloring within the lines will improve their child's hand-eye coordination. Yet so much of what a child does involves hand-eye coordination. When he picks up a raisin, puts together a puzzle, builds with blocks, or zips a zipper, he is improving his skills. He doesn't need a coloring book for practice.

Some parents believe that a child will learn to complete tasks if he works in a coloring book. But often, a child is unable successfully to stay within the lines of a coloring book picture, and becomes frustrated. A child between 3 and 5 may feel like a failure when he sees how "messy" his coloring looks: "I just can't do this." And parents may be more critical of their child's work when the task is to color within the lines rather than to draw whatever he likes. Eventually, the child may lose his interest in drawing and coloring: "I'm just not good at this."

Children are often given pre-done or partly completed artwork in nursery school or day care centers. They shouldn't then spend most of their arts and crafts time at home with pre-drawn coloring books. Parents should limit their child's use of coloring books until the child is at least 5 or 6 years old. At that age, he will be able to color within the lines and may find coloring books more satisfying. But even then, the use of coloring books should be limited.

The best kind of artwork for a child is the child's own. Your 3- to 5-year-old will enjoy using pens, pencils, markers, and crayons to color on blank paper. When he has a chance to draw what he likes, the drawing will be a part of him, and his pictures of people, animals, boats, and so on will be unique: "Look what I made!" Of course, some children are more interested in arts and crafts than others, and some will show more skill. But all children enjoy drawing if they feel successful. And as one 4½-year-old said, "When you draw and draw, you get better."

Keep art supplies available so your child can color when he wants to. He can draw on plain paper, scrap paper, the backs of computer printouts, newsprint, paper plates, lunch bags, grocery bags, etc. If you have a variety of pens and pencils, your child can pick the ones that are most comfortable to use. Many young children who have trouble drawing with crayons do much better with pens and markers.

My Child Wants to Play with Toy Guns

Many preschoolers—especially boys—want to play with guns. Children enjoy squirt guns, space guns, cap guns, and rifles, and they are impressed with what the guns can do: shoot water, flash, and make loud noises. If a gun isn't available, a child will make one out of wood, a stick, a straw, even paper. And if the child can't make one, he'll shoot with his thumb and finger.

A child is attracted to guns because they give him a sense of power and control. In his everyday life, the child is relatively helpless, but when he holds a toy gun (which looks real to him) he feels he can protect himself while telling other children what to do: "Stand over there or I'll kill you." Children like to play roles: fire fighter, mother, father, nurse, doctor, policeman, cowboy, bad guy. Children see shooting all the time on television, and they act out what they see. On TV, the good and bad guys have guns, and when the good guy shoots and wins, he's a hero.

There are many parents who are comfortable letting their children play with guns. Some parents even encourage it: "That's my boy!" Other parents have mixed feelings. They do not like gun play, since they know the danger and violence associated with real guns, and they prefer their children to play nonaggressively. But many of these parents eventually give up and let their children use guns. The parents find that, despite their logical arguments and their efforts to involve their child in other activities, the child still wants to play with guns, and if he can't buy one, he'll improvise one. Some parents relent because they don't feel strongly enough about the issue to struggle, while others feel they have no choice but to give in when their child is given a gun as a present.

You may decide not to let your child use toy guns, or to use them, but only in a limited way. You might tell him not to use his guns in the house, not to shoot at people who don't agree to play, and not to aim a toy gun in someone's face. Gun play may be difficult for you to watch, since it imitates an unpleasant part of life. Yet gun play seems to be part of a normal childhood, and it doesn't seem to encourage general aggressiveness. In fact, it can be an outlet for naturally aggressive children.

As long as your child plays with guns in moderation, there is no harm in the activity. He will probably stay interested in toy guns for many years, creating lengthy and elaborate shooting games (often based on themes or popular characters) as he goes through his elementary years. If you see gun play becoming your child's dominant form of play, try to figure out why. Does he feel unaccepted at home? Does he feel verbally or physically under attack at home or at school? A child who engages in excessive gun play may feel powerless or rejected. Try paying more attention to your child at home and try distracting him from guns by introducing him to alternative activities and organized games. You might see a real change in his play.

Should My Child Play with Children His Own Age?

All young children, even those under a year old, love to be around other children. When children 1½-years-old and younger play together, they usually get along well. They play side-by-side, independently engaged but enjoying each other's company, and there are few arguments over sharing. When there are occasional disagreements, they pass quickly because these young children can be easily distracted.

By the time children are 2 or 3 years old, however, playtime is full of arguments for playmates of the same age. They struggle with each other over possessions, sharing, and autonomy, and constantly shout, "That's mine!" A parent often has a difficult time watching children this age play together. They don't pay attention to each other's needs and don't give in without fighting. When children turn 4 they do get along better, although there is often a streak of competitiveness as each tries to exert power.

Play is generally much smoother when children of mixed ages play together. A group made up of 2- to 5-year-olds will struggle less because each child is at a different developmental stage and each has different needs. A younger child will watch and imitate an older one, asking for help with games and tasks, and getting information. An older child, who is less possessive, will give in to the younger ones, offering help, and leading games.

Although parents are usually comfortable when their young

child plays with an older friend, they are not as sure when their older child plays with a younger one. Parents may feel that their child will be bored with younger children, or will be brought down to their level. But a 5-year-old playing with 3-year-olds will stimulate himself, depending on the activities he's involved in: he will play elaborate games with the simple toys available, lead a complex game, or create his own arts and crafts projects. He might enjoy the chance to play again with toys he has outgrown. And he may feel good playing around younger children because he can be helpful and knowledgeable and because he can direct his friends' play: "Let's put the blocks here and build a village," "The puzzle piece goes there," "Do you want to hold my hamster? Be gentle, he has fragile bones." His own confidence will be boosted when he can teach and lead.

Sometimes there are problems with mixed age groups. An older child may engage in elaborate play that the younger child does not understand, and both children may become frustrated. And some older children may feel compelled to boss a younger child, knocking over his buildings and grabbing toys. When such children, who are usually re-enacting what happens to them when they play with an older sibling or friend, sense they are bigger than the children they are playing with, they try to exert power. Parental supervision is needed in such situations to keep the play between younger and older children peaceful.

When you arrange playtime for your young child, encourage him to choose playmates who seem right for him. At times you may find it works best when he plays with children his own age; at other times you may want him to practice relating to and accepting children of different ages. Most likely, your child will have some friends his own age and some older or younger. What is more important than the ages of playmates is how well the children get along together.

What About Playgroups?

Parents probably benefit from playgroups more than their children do. Parents of very young children often feel isolated, so they welcome a chance to meet with other adults, compare childrearing stories and advice, and observe how other parents handle their children. Of course the children also can benefit from a playgroup, and as they get older, they enjoy seeing their friends regularly and playing at each other's homes.

If you are interested in starting a playgroup, talk to other parents about the possibility. Ask your neighbors and friends or look in grocery stores, churches, synagogues, and newsletters for notices from other interested parents. Although playgroups are most convenient when the participants live near each other, groups often form between people in different neighborhoods.

Your playgroup will probably work best with three to five children of mixed ages. If all the children are 2½, there will be a great deal of arguing over possessions, but if some are 2 and some are 4, group meetings will be more harmonious. The youngest child will be happy playing alone next to the others, and the oldest ones will be more likely than the 2-year-olds to share toys.

Many playgroups are successful meeting in the morning, although some meet between 3:30 and 5:30 in the afternoon, normally a slow time for families with young children. Other playgroups meet on the weekends so parents who work full time can participate.

Your playgroup will probably get together once a week, meeting at each member's house in turn. In some groups, every parent comes every time, while in others, parents rotate attendance so that in a group with six children, two parents attend any one session while four have the time free. The success of this rotating method depends on the ages and personalities of the children, and how well the families know each other. Some young children do not want to be separated from their parents and may cry for 5 minutes or for the whole play session, particularly if the parents in charge are not familiar.

Before your playgroup begins meeting, get together with the other parents involved and develop rules and standards for practical issues. What kind of snack will be served? What happens when children fight? Who should bring toys? How will you handle the problem of sharing toys?

Your playgroup will be most successful if the parents involved share similar interests and attitudes, especially regarding parenting, since conflicts can arise when one group member accepts behavior that bothers another. As long as the adult members of a playgroup are basically compatible, they will be able to talk about their differences and work out solutions to the group's problems.

My Child Likes to Talk
on the Telephone

Children like to do what their parents do, and parents spend a lot of time on the telephone. Even before a child is 2 years old, he will imitate his parents by using a toy phone, holding a real phone, pushing the buttons, and making sounds. When he is between 2 and 3, he will want to talk on the phone and given the chance, he may do comical things. He might listen and nod without saying a word, or he may hold objects up to the phone so his listener can see them since he assumes that if he can see something, everyone else can. One 2-year-old had his aunt hold on while he got his pet gerbil. "See," he said, holding the animal up to the receiver, "he's moving around."

Children like to imitate their parents by being first to answer the phone. Parents who want to avoid this situation shout, "I'll get it," but sometimes their child also shouts, "I'll get it," and races his parents to the phone. When a 2-year-old answers the phone, he might just hold it, saying nothing. A 3-year-old might pick up the phone and say, "Who is this?" or "What do you want?" and a 4- or 5-year-old who is given a message by a caller will probably forget it.

Children are fascinated by the telephone not only because their parents use it, but also because it has a magical quality. It is both tool and toy, and it lets a child share his thoughts with other people, something children like to do. Children also like to talk on the phone because they don't want to feel left out. If parents are having a conversation, children want to be in on it and they want the attention their parents are giving to whoever is on the line.

Parents are often frustrated when their child wants to talk, especially when they are engaged in important calls. A child might yell and have a tantrum if he is not allowed to talk, and such noise can embarrass parents. If a child becomes too disruptive, his parent might have to end an important call prematurely, hoping that the person on the other end is understanding. Although parents can gradually teach a 4- or 5-year-old not to interrupt important calls, explanations do little good with younger, egocentric children. Sometimes these children can be distracted by a silent offer of toys, crayons, or food, but more often they just keep interrupting.

Parents may feel particularly embarrassed if their child answers an important phone call. One mother expected a business call from a man named Paul Jones. Her son picked up the phone, listened, and then shouted, "It's Paul Bones. Who's he?" A 4-year-old can be taught to answer the phone politely, but parents of younger children have to be tolerant and hope their callers have an understanding of children's behavior and a sense of humor.

One way you can accommodate your young child's desire to answer the phone is to ask relatives or friends to call your child at pre-arranged times; then you can safely let him answer the phone and talk. If you have an understanding adult who enjoys making such calls, you may be able to keep your child from interrupting you. Tell him, "As soon as I'm off the phone, we'll dial Aunt Ellen and ask her to give you a call."

If you are having a phone conversation with the parent of a child the same age as yours, ask if your child can talk for a few moments. The other parent will certainly understand and may want to put his or her own child on to talk to you. And since children like to talk to each other, your child may especially enjoy a chance to call one of his friends.

My Child Gets Anxious Before
Holidays and Her Birthday

"How long 'til my birthday?" "When is three weeks up?" "Is it Halloween yet?" Parents hear such questions whenever special occasions approach. Children have a hard time waiting, and since their concept of time is different from an adult's, they ask about holidays over and over again. Parents can tell their excited child that Christmas is four weeks away and almost immediately, the child will ask again, "How long before Christmas?"

A child begins anticipating a holiday as soon as pre-holiday preparations begin. The child's nursery school class might make valentines weeks in advance, and her friends might discuss Halloween costumes long before October. Christmas preparations sometimes begin before Thanksgiving, giving children a great deal of time to watch holiday commercials, see store decorations going up, and think about presents.

When there is a long period of anticipation before a special event, children get anxious and excited, and may go through behavior changes, becoming sillier, more active, and more likely to whine. Children who are admonished to "be good" in order to get birthday or Christmas gifts may feel pressured and become more aggressive. It is very hard under any circumstances for a child to be consistently good, and when the child is anxiously anticipating a holiday, behaving well is that much harder. Some parents find that their child's behavior improves if they ease up on the holiday pressure, perhaps giving a surprise treat ("Just because I love you") to slow the build-up of expectations.

Parents can also try to help their child deal with the waiting period by giving her a calendar to mark off, or by making a special paper chain. Each day for a week or two, the child can tear off one chain; the day all the chains are gone is the day the child has been waiting for. These devices help some children stay calm, but generally children remain very excited. They want the celebration to begin "now." Parents can sympathize if they consider their own feelings before special parties or vacations. Adult anticipation can also be strong for weeks.

Your child may get particularly worked up before her birthday. Since party preparation takes time, you may start planning the birthday weeks before the date, while your child considers whom to invite and what presents she would like. She may be very excited about the gifts and party or she may have mixed feelings about being the center of attention and may decide, as one 5-year-old did, "Nobody should sing 'Happy Birthday' to me at my party." Your child may worry ahead of time about having eight or ten friends over at once, and may be concerned about sharing her toys and letting the guests see her presents. One child, concerned about her anticipated gifts, said, "At the party, no one can come and play in my room." Although there is no way to keep your child from feeling excited and anxious before her birthday, if you anticipate her feelings, you will be better able to reassure her about her concerns.

My Child Doesn't Want
to Share

"It's mine!" screams the young boy, yanking a toy from another child.

"That's not nice," his mother says. "Michelle is your friend and I want you to share with her."

"No, it's mine!"

At times almost all young children have trouble sharing. Even 18-month-olds argue over toys, although conflicts generally peak between the ages of 2 and 3. Episodes of screaming, crying, and even biting are not uncommon when children struggle for a toy. Sometimes the severity of the anger and anxiety that young children exhibit is incomprehensible to adults. One mother who took care of several young children described her daughter's behavior during this stage as horrifying. "When Tali was 2 she would stand at the front door with her arms spread out and yell, MINE!"

What parents should try to understand is that a child's possessions are important to him and that he feels violated if another child handles them. When a friend comes into a child's home, the child is suddenly asked to give up his toys, to share with someone who usually doesn't ask before using something. The child's biggest fear is that he will lose his toys, or that they will no longer belong to him. That's why he screams and tugs at a possession, crying, "It's mine!"

Because a young child's thinking is egocentric, he sees things only from his own point of view, and is unmoved by his parents' logical reasons for sharing. "Your friend wants to use this toy. How would you feel if he didn't share with you?" The question is a good one, but it probably won't change the child's behavior. The child also won't be moved by his friend's obvious distress at not having a chance to share a toy. One 3½-year-old child became interested in her toy vacuum cleaner only after her friend took it out of the closet to use. A struggle ensued between the two children until the mother intervened. "Jesse was using the toy first. How would you feel if your friend Niki took her toys away from you while you were visiting her?" The child stood quietly with a blank look on her face and said, "It's my vacuum cleaner." Such lack of concern for another's feelings may be difficult for parents to accept because adult thinking is so different from a young child's.

Parents who are frustrated or embarrassed by their child's unwillingness to share may blame themselves or have negative feelings about their child, considering him to be bad or selfish. After watching their child grab a toy, parents may become angry and try to force him to share. But once parents realize that trouble with sharing is a normal aspect of development, they usually feel more comfortable and tolerant. Talking to other parents about sharing may also help a parent feel better. It is helpful to remember that sometimes even adults have problems sharing. People argue over parking spaces and cut each other off during rush hour. And an adult need only imagine a visiting friend opening drawers and looking at personal belongings to understand how a child feels about sharing.

Understanding your child's difficulty with sharing may bring some comfort, although you will still have to deal with struggles over toys. Unfortunately there are no magic answers to the problems of sharing, but there are things you can try to lessen the tension. First, you can prepare your child. If a friend is coming to visit, try saying, "When Michelle comes over she will want to play with your blocks, your puzzles, and your sliding board." You can also ask Michelle's parents to send along a little bag of toys for your child to play with. Don't expect your child to share all his toys when a friend visits. You may want to put away a few special possessions, or explain to visitors that there are some toys your child does not want to share.

If your child grabs everything away from his friend, tell him, "Michelle is using that now, and when she's finished, you may use it." Then tell Michelle, "When you're done with that toy, please share it." Sometimes you may want to set time limits for taking turns, although this will mean playing referee. When the struggle over toys becomes intense, you can try to interest your child in playing with another toy. Or it may help to offer him choices: "Which toy would you like your friend to use—the ball or the puzzle?" If you child can't choose, tell him that his friend will decide. You may have to distract your child by playing with him yourself or reading him a book. Although this can be frustrating, especially if you are involved in conversation with another adult, you should recognize that conflicts among young children, and the resulting interruptions, are unavoidable.

Parents often find that sharing is easier if children play outside, if they play at a friend's house rather than at their own house, or if children are involved in something together, such as coloring, using play dough, or painting. Whatever you try, though, sharing will probably still be a problem for your young child. As you set limits on the struggles, reassure your child and let him know you understand what a difficult time he is having. And remember to model the behavior you want him to adopt. If you are giving, if you share courteously, your child will eventually copy you. Children learn more from parents' examples than from parents' admonitions.

By the time your child is 3 or 4 years old, you will notice a general change in his attitude toward sharing. He will show less anxiety when a friend uses a toy, and will begin to say, "Here, you use this," or "Let's both play with these." When he is 4 or 5, he will begin to place more value on friendship than on possessions. Eventually your child may be sharing more openly than you would like, and you may find yourself saying, "Don't let him use your bike; he might ruin it," or "Don't let her take that toy home with her."

In the meantime, you can help your young child get past his difficulty with sharing by understanding the problem and by not applying too much pressure. All parents want their children to be giving people, and with patience, you will see your child develop his ability to share with others.

How Do Other Children Act
When They Are Angry
with Each Other?

"Katie, let's play house. I'm the mommy, you're the baby."

"No, I'm the mommy, or I won't be your friend."

"Then you're not coming to my birthday party."

This exchange is typical of what preschoolers say when they argue. They may play well together and then suddenly tell each other, "I hate you," or "You're a dummy." Young children, whose emotions are close to the surface, concentrate on their immediate wishes and needs. And because children are egocentric, they do not consider each other's feelings, but let their anger come out in harsh words or actions. Some children give in when spoken to harshly by another child, while others either fight back and persist until they get their way, or try to find an adult to help them.

Parents wonder what to do when children are angry with each other. Parents should first let children try to work out their differences themselves, as long as no one is getting physically hurt or having his or her feelings terribly hurt. Children are often surprisingly good at settling their arguments. If parents intervene too soon, their child may not learn how to work problems out with another child, and may become a "tattle tale," dependent on her parents for help even with minor difficulties.

Parents who see that their children cannot resolve an argument alone should offer suggestions: "Why don't you both pretend you're mommies and let your dolls be the babies?" If children are speaking too harshly, parents can ask, "Is there another way to tell her what you want?" Or they can suggest that, rather than call names, their child say to her friend, "I don't like it when you —." Even if angry children ignore these suggestions, the very presence of parents will have a restraining effect. Children tend to be less aggressive with each other when adults are nearby.

If your child is arguing a lot, you will probably place limits on her behavior because you don't want her to hurt someone else, physically or emotionally. But if you restrict your child's expressions of anger too much, she may end up believing that anger is a bad and inappropriate emotion. When she is kept from expressing her feelings, they will be released in other ways. She may become destructive with her toys or while playing; manipulative with you or her friends; or tricky as she tries to get other children to do what she wants. She needs a chance to let her anger out and even if you don't like to hear her say,

"I hate you! I'm not playing with you," you should realize that children are not very good at expressing their exact thoughts. Harsh words are sometimes a young child's way of letting her strongest negative feelings be known.

Try to avoid situations that usually lead to children's arguments. For instance, your child may play well with one child at a time, but not when a third child joins in. Three is a bad number: two friends will often pair up and exclude or attack the third. If you can't avoid this situation, give all three children frequent reminders about getting along and including each other in play. If your child consistently argues with one particular playmate, limit their time together or tell them, "You have to find a way to get along with each other or I'm not going to allow you to play together." Your young child's anger, no matter how momentary, is very real and very strong. Allow her emotions to be heard, but when necessary, help her control her anger by setting firm limits.

BEING NICE

My Child is Uncomfortable Kissing Relatives

In most families, children are expected to kiss their relatives hello and goodbye. When a child does this spontaneously his parents are pleased, and when he doesn't, they usually prompt him: "Go give Aunt Jody a kiss. She hasn't seen you in such a long time." Parents are often anxious to have their child give kisses. They know how nice it feels to be kissed by a child, they want their child to be liked by relatives, and they feel that they will be judged unfavorably if their child doesn't give a kiss.

Yet many children are uncomfortable kissing their relatives and often don't want to do it. This can create an awkward situation, especially when a relative feels rejected by the child or feels that the child is not excited to see her. And if the relative has brought the child a gift and still doesn't get a kiss, she might feel particularly frustrated and begin to say negative things about the child. "What's the matter with him? Is he shy?" The child's uneasy parents may urge him to "Give Aunt Sue a kiss since she gave you a present," and Aunt Sue may say, "I'll take my gift back home with me." All of this can put a great deal of pressure on the young child, who will usually give in if harassed enough. But the resulting discomfort for the parent and child is often not worth the struggle.

A child who resists giving a kiss is probably not rejecting a relative. Most children are excited about seeing family members, but feel uneasy giving a kiss hello for any of a number of reasons. A child may just not be comfortable with the physical contact of a kiss, or, feeling shy and self-conscious, he may reject kissing because he does not like to be focused on. He may want to stay close to his parents, even cling to them, until he feels adjusted to the visitors or to being in a relative's house.

Sometimes a relative is one the child rarely sees, and the child resists kissing because he needs time to get used to a strange face. A few children have private or magical concerns about kissing. One 5-year-old worried that he would "turn old" if he kissed his aunt, while another child reported that she did not want to kiss her relatives because "people give you germs on your lips." And at times a child won't give a kiss goodbye because he does not want a visit to end, although he may not explain this.

If you are faced with a resisting child, try to let the kiss go— most children just need time to ease into a visit and feel friendly. Instead of insisting on a kiss, suggest other options for your child. He could tell his relatives about something that has recently happened, demonstrate a new skill, or show them a favorite possession. And a child who won't kiss may willingly "give five," shake hands, blow a kiss, or give a hug goodbye.

We can all remember being small and having a relative pinch our cheeks or demand a kiss. If we recall how we felt then, we can understand our own children's reluctance to give kisses, and we can help them find other ways to begin and end enjoyable visits with relatives.

Is It All Right for Her to Call Me by My First Name?

It is very common for a first-born child between the ages of 18 months and 3 years to call her parents by their first names. The child imitates what she hears and since her parents and their friends, neighbors, and relatives all use first names when talking to each other, the child uses first names too. Even if the parents call each other "Mom" and "Dad," the child may still use first names because those are the ones she hears most often.

Many parents don't mind if their child occasionally uses first names, although some parents consider anything other than "Mom" and "Dad" disrespectful. When a child uses her parents' first names, however, she intends no disrespect—usually she is just mimicking what other people say. Over time, this imitative behavior will diminish and the child will almost certainly stop using her parents' names.

If you are bothered or embarrassed when your child calls you by your first name, remind her to say "Mom" and "Dad." But remember that it will be hard for her, especially if she is under 2, to call you "Mom" and "Dad" consistently, since she doesn't usually hear other people call you that. If you have a second child, you will notice that he or she rarely uses your first name. That is because there is an older sibling to copy, and because the second child is used to hearing "Mom" and "Dad."

A common question related to first-name use is, "What

should my child's friends call me?" Some parents are most comfortable with first names and believe they are easier for young children to remember and use. Other parents want to be called "Mrs." or "Mr." Choose whichever makes you comfortable and let your child's playmates know what you would like to be called.

What Can I Do About My Child's Whining?

Hearing a child whine is very annoying. Young children often whine when they are tired, hungry, angry, or frustrated, and once they start, it is difficult to stop them. When parents ignore their whining child, he usually just continues to whine until they finally speak to him. And even those parents who try to be patient, or who believe it is best not to focus on a whining child, often end up shouting, "Stop whining!" One mother constantly scolded her 4-year-old, "What did I tell you about whining! Use a grown-up voice!"

There are no easy ways to keep your child from whining. You can try redirecting his attention, although your attempts at distraction may often be unsuccessful. You can also try letting him know, without attacking him, that you are unhappy with his tone. When you say, "You're whining!" or "Stop whining!" you imply blame. Instead, try expressing your feelings in a less negative way, without using the word "whining" at all. You can say, "When you ask me in that way, I don't want to do anything for you," or "You'll have to ask me in another way."

Sometimes, particularly if your child is 3 or younger, you won't be able to understand what he says when he whines. You can tell him, "You'll have to ask me in a voice I can understand," or "When you talk to me that way, I don't feel like listening to you. Can you find another way to tell me what you want?" You may not be able to stop a 3-year-old's whining until

215

you discover what is causing it. Sometimes a child with an older sibling whines because he feels he can't compete with his brother or sister. He turns to whining and baby-talk in order to be noticed and to take on the qualities of a baby, who, he feels, couldn't be expected to act like the older sibling.

By the time your child is 5 he should be better able to express himself and to understand the limits you place on his whining. If he seems to whine continuously despite your efforts to curtail his whining, it may be a sign that he needs more attention or that he believes whining is a way to get what he wants. If you let your child know that he will not get his way when he whines, he may decide that whining is not worth the trouble.

"I Hate You, Mommy!"
"Daddy, You Dummy!"

When a young child gets angry with her parents, she shouts, "I hate you. You're dumb!" This outburst might come after the child's parents have said she can't go outdoors or have a friend over or do something else she wants to do. A preschooler has a hard time putting her exact feelings into words. She doesn't know how to say, "Dad, I think you should allow me to stay up later tonight because . . ." or "I'm angry with you because you said . . ." She's too young for such articulation and too young to show respect. Instead, she expresses her anger by saying, "I hate you."

Most preschool children say "I hate you" to their parents. Some parents accept and understand these words as the beginning of their child's expression of angry, negative feelings. But all parents can feel betrayed when their child, after receiving love and attention, turns on them over a minor disappointment. It can be frustrating when adult reasoning, logic and caring fail to keep a child from yelling, "You mean Mom." Many parents are tolerant when their 2- or 3-year-old yells, "You dumb Mom," but feel much less understanding when their 4- or 5-year-old says, "I hate you." A child's words can feel threatening to parents who don't like their children to be angry with them.

Parents who cannot stand to hear their child say "I hate you" often say, "That's not nice! Don't let me hear those words again." But the child needs to release her angry feelings somehow, and if she isn't allowed to express them verbally, she will find other, perhaps more destructive ways to vent her feelings. She might turn to aggressive behavior such as biting or hitting, or she might take out her anger in hidden ways: she may become deliberately slow, act excessively silly, pretend she doesn't hear her parents, or find other ways to annoy them. However, if the child's angry feelings are acknowledged and allowed to be expressed, the child will eventually learn to express her feelings more appropriately.

If "I hate you" bothers you, offer your child (particularly if she is 4 or 5) other ways to tell how she feels. Suggest she say, "I'm mad at you," or "I'm angry with you," or "I don't like what you did." Acknowledge her feelings by saying, "I know you're angry with me, but I want you to tell me in different words."

Children are natural mimics. Your child uses the word "hate" because she hears it so often. Adults say, "I hate this dress," or "I hate it when people do that." It is natural for your child to use the word to express her dislike of something or someone. You can take advantage of the fact that she is a mimic and gradually teach her to express her anger in acceptable ways. When your child says, "I hate you," rather than make an issue of it, simply re-state her words. Say back to her, "You're really angry at me, aren't you. You don't like it when I say it's time to come in." If your child hears you express her anger in this way, she gradually will begin to use similar statements herself.

How Can I Teach My Child to Respect Others?

There are two ways a child learns about respect. He listens to what his parents say about respectful behavior, and he copies the way his parents actually act. Ultimately, he will learn more from his parents' actions than from their words. If his parents treat him with respect, and if he sees them act courteously to others, he will eventually copy their behavior. But if his parents speak harshly to him—"Get over here now!"—and consistently belittle him when he expresses his needs or makes mistakes, he will not learn to treat others with respect, even if his parents admonish him to behave well.

A child is most likely to be respectful of others if his parents treat him with respect and also remind him to treat others well. Nursery school teachers sometimes say they can tell how respectful parents are by listening to children playing in the housekeeping corner. When two preschoolers pretend they have a crying baby, one might say, "Let's pick her up. She's crying," while the other might reply, "You get out of this house right now and take this crying baby with you."

A young child doesn't automatically know how to act appropriately. He has to have good models and be taught and reminded, because he is egocentric and easily forgets about other people's feelings when his own needs are strong. Parents often feel defeated after telling their child again and again to be nice to others, only to see him act selfishly again. At such times,

219

parents should remember that learning to show respect is a slow process and that it is natural for young children to think mainly of themselves.

If you feel constantly unhappy with your child's disrespectful behavior, perhaps you should re-evaluate your expectations. It is possible that you are asking for more than he is capable of. The younger your child, the less likely he is to control his emotions and put himself in someone else's place.

Look for ways you can model respectful behavior and ways you can show respect to your child: "Let me pick you up so you can see better," "Let's go over there and thank that man for helping us." When children are respected, they internalize feelings of self-worth, believing that their ideas, needs, and desires are important. Over time, your child will give back the kind of respect you have given him, and you will see him begin to consider other people's needs and feelings.

Should I Ask My Child to Say "Please" and "Thank You"?

"Jennifer, how do you ask for something?" "Now what do you say to Aunt Marie?" "What's the magic word?" A child who is questioned like this may mumble a faint "please" or "thank you," and her parents may feel somewhat reassured. But they may also wonder why they have to constantly remind her to use polite words.

When children say "please" and "thank you" without being prompted or coerced, parents feel a sense of satisfaction. They are proud when their child is polite in public, and they feel good when she is polite at home. Children make so many requests throughout the day: "Get me a drink!" "Give me a napkin!" "Tie my shoe!" If a child prefaces these statements with "please" and remembers to say "thank you," her parents will not feel so overwhelmed and will usually have an easier time responding to her constant needs.

So why don't most young children say please and thank you spontaneously? And why do many parents find themselves in situations such as this: a mother preparing to leave a neighborhood party tells her 3-year-old daughter, "Say 'goodbye' and 'thank you' to Mrs. Miller." The child turns away and refuses to speak as seven mothers stare at her. The mother tries again, then thanks the hostess herself and leaves, feeling defeated and embarrassed by her child's impoliteness.

Yet when children forget or refuse to say "please" and "thank you" they are usually not being impolite. There are several explanations for their behavior. First, young children have a difficult time grasping general rules, including ones about responding in socially appropriate ways. A child who is told to say "thank you" when given something at Grandma's house may not connect that experience to a similar one that happens later at a neighbor's house. Although the child is again being given something, she is too young to understand that she should respond as she did earlier.

Another reason children may not use polite words is shyness. While some children respond to prompting, others are just too self-conscious, especially when adult attention is focused on them. A shy child may refuse to say "please" or "thank you," and this can lead to a struggle if her parents try to force the issue.

Finally, a child may be too preoccupied to say "please" and "thank you," especially if she has just been given a new toy, or if she has an urgent request. A young child has a difficult time thinking about and considering other people's wishes, and saying what her parents want her to say may be the furthest thing from her mind when she's excited.

Sometimes parents who frequently remind their child to say "please" set up a bind for themselves. They may inadvertently convince their child that all her wishes will be granted if she uses what, for her, may actually seem like a magic word. For example, a child in a toy store may say, "Please, Mom, please. Will you buy this for me?" Since the child has said "please," she feels she should get what she's asking for. When her parents explain why she can't have the toy she politely asked for, the child may not understand (or not want to hear) her parents' reasoning. And the parents can find themselves in a dilemma. Since they want to encourage politeness, they may be reluctant to say "no" when their child is saying "please." In such a situation, the child receives a confusing mixed message: saying "please" sometimes gets her what she's asked for, but often doesn't.

If your child does not often say "please" and "thank you" on her own, there are a number of things you can try doing. You can watch for the times when she does use polite words and reinforce that behavior by saying, "I really like the way you asked for that." If you know that your child is too shy to say "thank you," you can do the thanking for her, which may make you both more comfortable, and let you model polite behavior for her. And if you are unhappy with the way your child has asked for something, you can say, "When you ask me that way, it doesn't make me want to give you anything," or "You'll have to find another way of asking." Such statements give your child an opportunity to say "please" or to change her tone of voice.

Tone can be very important. As adults, we are usually more concerned about using a polite tone than about always attaching "please" to our own requests. When your child makes frequent demands ("Zip my jacket!") you may be so frustrated with her tone that you find yourself harshly demanding politeness ("PLEASE!"). If your child mimics that harsh "please," you still won't like the way she sounds. But if, instead of demanding a "please," you model the right tone for your child, she may understand what you want and respond using a pleasant tone of voice.

Finally, remember to say "please" and "thank you" to your child when you ask her for something, when she does what you've asked, and when she brings you something. All too often we make requests and demands of children without ever saying "please" and "thank you" to them. When your child hears you speaking politely to her and to other children and adults, she will begin to do as you do, and increasingly you will hear her saying "please" and "thank you" on her own.

Sometimes I Want My Child to Say "I'm Sorry"

A mother who sees her son hit his playmate says, "That wasn't nice. Now tell your friend you're sorry." The boy reluctantly mumbles "sorry" but it is clear he feels no remorse. In fact, he probably believes he did nothing wrong. Young children are egocentric and often focus on fulfilling their own needs, without considering other people's feelings. At times, young children grab, hit, knock over each other's blocks, say unkind things, and refuse to share. Parents who don't want their child to do these things should set firm limits on inappropriate behavior, rather than coerce their child into making insincere apologies.

When a child is forced to apologize, and when saying "I'm sorry" is the main consequence for unacceptable behavior, the child may decide that it is worth hitting other children or knocking over their toys. All he has to do is apologize afterwards and he may be excused without punishment or further consequence.

Parents often enforce an apology because it is a quick and easy way to deal with misbehavior. Yet parents know that hearing their child say "I'm sorry" can at times be unsatisfying, particularly if the child has done something dangerous such as throw sand in a playmate's face. Parents may try to talk to their child about his unacceptable action and the child may respond, "But I already said I'm sorry." However, when parents don't emphasize apologies, their child can't so easily "get off the hook." He has to find other ways to resolve conflicts.

The real motivation for a child to change his behavior comes not from the fear of having to apologize, but from the fear of disappointing and angering his parents and, as he gets older, his friends. A child who doesn't want his parents to get angry at him may apologize on his own for misbehavior. Such an apology comes from within the child and is much more sincere than an apology the child is forced to make.

Parents may wonder why their child doesn't make sincere apologies more often. Sometimes he is too embarrassed or ashamed to admit wrongdoing and at other times he may not like being put on the spot. A child may deny his actions ("I didn't do it!") either because he actually believes it's true or because he fears his parents' reactions and disapproval. Often, young children have strong feelings of autonomy and resist doing what their parents want them to do: "No! I won't say I'm sorry."

When your child hurts another child, focus on setting limits. Rather than say, "You hit her, now apologize," say "I'm not going to allow you to hit her," or "You may not want to play with her, but I'm not going to let you hurt her." If your child is 4 or 5 years old, have him help remedy a situation. "Since you pushed over your friend's blocks, you have to help her put her building back together." You can also model considerate behavior for your child by apologizing for him. "I'm sorry he pushed over your building. He's going to help you build it again."

The older your child gets, the more easily you can discuss angry feelings with him. Listen to your child's reasons for misbehavior, no matter how far-fetched they seem. Before your child can offer sincere apologies, he needs to believe that he can explain his side of a disagreement. Children (and adults) who feel unheard often defend themselves and, unless coerced, refuse to apologize even when they know they are wrong.

Since your child imitates your behavior, remember to apologize to him when you overreact, bump into him, or take him away from play to rush out for your own reasons. If you apologize whenever the situation calls for it, your child will eventually copy your words and actions.

What About Bathroom Language?

"Billy, what are you going to be for Halloween?" asks Jane.

"Doo doo face," says Billy, and both children laugh.

Young children think it's funny to say such words as doo doo, pee pee, boobies, and butt. The words are not quite "bad," but to children they have power. Children use bathroom language when they feel silly or when they need a quick way to be funny and make their friends laugh. The words also provide a way of releasing tension and getting attention. A child might use bathroom words more than usual when there is a new baby in her family, when she is unhappy in school, or when she wants the attention of a friend who is playing with someone else. Using these words often does bring a child instant attention from adults and friends.

Different parents have different reactions to bathroom language. Some parents just shrug their shoulders and ignore the words. Others are annoyed or embarrassed and wonder where their child learned such langauge. They worry that their child will be reprimanded by a teacher or caretaker, and wonder if their child's use of bathroom language is a reflection on their parenting.

You should feel reassured to know that all children use bathroom words, which they hear and repeat on the playground. It is almost impossible to delete the words from your child's vocabulary. The best you can do, if you are bothered, is put limits on where and when your child may use bathroom words. "I don't want you to talk that way while we are at the dinner table," or simply, "I really don't want to listen to you using those words right now." But don't dwell on the fact that the child is using "bad" words. Rather, keep reminding her that these words may create problems for her with other people who get upset at such language.

My Child Uses Profanity

Parents often forget that children are active listeners and imitators. If parents use profanity (and most do, either regularly or during moments of anger), so will their children. And children are surprisingly good mimics. They swear with their parents' tone and intensity, and they use curse words in the appropriate contexts. Young children pick up profanity, which they also hear from playmates, just as they pick up other phrases.

When people respond with surprise to a child who has used a curse word, or when they say, "That's bad," the child learns that profanity has power. The child may continue to use swear words to test out their shock value and to try to understand what makes certain words bad. Although it is hard for parents not to respond, if the child gets little or no reaction to his swearing, he will soon stop.

Parents are usually alarmed by their child's swearing. They fear embarrassment and they worry that their child will be blamed for teaching profanity to other children. Parents also fear that their child's cursing will reflect on the entire family, and that people may assume such language is used and condoned in the child's home. Because of these fears, many parents become angry and react strongly when their child uses profanity. But parents should be careful not to blame their child for his natural tendency to imitate what he hears.

If your child uses swear words only occasionally, there is no need to be concerned. But if he uses such words often, or if the words bother you a great deal, there are several things you can do. The most important is to stop using profanity yourself. If your child no longer hears the words, he will probably stop saying them. You can also explain that you do not want him using profanity, and you can set firm limits on his language. Finally, you can wait a while; most young children give up profanity once the novelty wears off, although during the elementary years they may experiment with profanity again.

I Want My Children to Get Along with Each Other

Family dynamics change drastically when a second child is born. While parents give constant care to their infant, their older child often reacts negatively because of the major adjustments she has to make. Reactions vary, of course, with the age of the older sibling: a 4- or 5-year-old will be much more independent and understanding than a 1- to 3-year-old, but all older siblings will have some negative feelings. The way parents respond to their older child's feelings about the baby often sets the tone for the children's future relationship.

Some parents, who pressure their older child to love the baby, try to censure their child's feelings: "Don't say that about your little brother—it's not nice," "Be gentle with the baby." A child who is not allowed to share her negative feelings with her parents will continue to have those feelings; she will just express them in other ways. She may not take her anger out on her parents since she, like all young children, fears losing their love, but she may take her anger out on her sibling.

The older child needs the freedom to express her negative feelings so she can resolve them. If her parents allow her to say, "Take the baby back to the hospital," and show that they understand her situation by saying, "It's sometimes hard, isn't it, to have a new baby in the house. Mommy and Daddy can't give you all the attention we used to, but we love you and know how you feel," the child will be reassured. She will begin to accept and even like the baby once she knows that she can express her dislike without risking her parents' love. The more the older child is accepted and reassured, the more likely she is to develop positive feelings about her sibling, although there will always be some negative feelings as well.

Your older child will begin to feel good about her sibling when the baby starts smiling, giggling, and seeking her out. "He likes me!" You should support and encourage this early interaction by saying, "Yes, he really does like you. He seems to think you're funny and nice." At this point, the older sibling might enjoy helping you take care of the baby.

As your children grow, you will have to consciously encourage them to respect each other. When they show consideration, give them positive feedback. "That was nice of you to pick up his toy," "Thanks for helping her put the puzzle together." If you treat each of your children with love, and show that you accept them and their similarities and differences, they will respond positively.

Don't make one child seem more important or more deserving of consideration than the other. If you say, "Let him do it—he's younger," or "She's older, so she can go," or "She's better at it, so let her go first," you will give your children reasons to feel resentful and jealous, and you will encourage a cycle of competitiveness. And if you say, "The baby needs to be carried, but you're big enough to walk," or "Don't play with the baby's toys. You're too old for that," your older child will feel anger that will be directed at her younger sibling, not at you.

At times you may sympathize with your older child, but be careful not to encourage her negative feelings. Listen to her complaints about her younger sibling but don't say, "Yes, he really is a nuisance, isn't he." Your older child will consider your comments a license to feel and say what she wants about her sibling, and your younger child may end up feeling rejected.

Be matter-of-fact about the different things you do with your children. "She's going to bed later because she slept later this morning," or "I'm putting this together for him because he doesn't understand how to do it." If your children are four or more years apart, there will be many times when you treat your children differently. The older one will be allowed to watch a special television show or stay outside by herself while the younger one will not. In such cases, don't present the older child's activities as "better," or as privileges, since your younger child will interpret the privileges to mean, "She's better than I am." Discourage your children from feeling competitive about what they are allowed to do. Rather, let both children know "This is just the way things are right now." Each child does what is appropriate.

When your older child wants to play alone or with friends, you may have to distract your younger child by reading to him or having one of his friends over. The older child needs her privacy and her possessions, but at times she also has to give in and let her younger sibling join in the play. You may be tempted, if your children are four or more years apart, to make the older one responsible for entertaining her sibling. However, this is unfair to the older one, who may resent having someone "follow me around all the time." Forcing one child to stay with the other will probably increase the bad feelings between your children.

If your children are one to three years apart, they will share many of the same interests, toys, and friends, a situation that can lead to conflict. When a friend comes to play, encourage the children to include everyone. The child who brought the friend can have more control over the games, but siblings should be allowed to play. Although the child who must share her friend may be resentful at first, she will soon focus on playing. If you let one of your children exclude the other from all play, the one left out will develop strong negative feelings about his sibling.

If your children are close in age and argue over toys, try to downplay the issue of possession. Rather than say, "That's his toy," encourage your children to share and trade their playthings, and provide some toys that will interest both. If your younger child wants to play with something that belongs to his sibling, distract the older child for a moment so the younger has a chance with the toy. Then thank your older child for sharing, even though she did not do so intentionally. Similarly, distract the younger child so you can return his sister's toy, and tell him, "Isn't it nice she let you play with this for a little while."

In spite of all you do to encourage a good relationship, your children will still argue with each other, probably some every day. Allow them to work out their own problems as much as possible and try not to take sides. Too often parents end up blaming quarrels on the older child "who should know better." When this happens, the older child gets angry at her parents for scolding her, but she takes out her anger on her sibling because he is a safer target. Try to understand and accept the arguments—they are inevitable. And take comfort and pleasure in the times you see your children showing genuine love and consideration for each other.

How Can I Teach My Child to Be Gentle with His Pet?

It is not unusual for a young child to handle his pet roughly and play with it in inappropriate ways. He may touch its eyes, pull its fur, put his fingers in its ears, and even sit on it. One child carried her hamster in her purse; another child was delighted to let his pet gerbil "have fun rolling down the steps."

Parents frequently react to such mistreatment by saying, "How would you like it if someone did that to you?" One veterinarian became so irritated by the way his daughter carried the family's new dog that he carried his daughter around the same way to show her what such treatment felt like. However, logic and examples have little effect on children under 5, who have a difficult time putting themselves in another person's (or pet's) place.

A child doesn't mean to cause harm when he mishandles his pet. He just intends to play with it and explore it, and he doesn't understand the consequences of his actions. In fact, most children are very fond of their pets, and some children develop strong emotional attachments to them, since pets can serve as comforting companions. One child, seeking acceptance after his father disciplined him, hugged his cat and said, "You like me, you're my friend." Children often share feelings with their pets. "Mommy won't let me go outside and I want to."

Your child may feel a great deal of affection for his pet, but if your child is under 5 years old, you have probably seen him mistreat the animal. In order to protect the pet, show your child exactly how to handle it and be prepared to remind him often about appropriate holding and touching. You may also have to set consequences: "If you handle the dog roughly, you will not be allowed to play with him."

If your child is 4 or 5 years old, a lesson with consistent reminders and firm limits should work, but if he is 3 or under, he is too young to remember how to play with a pet safely. Therefore, you will have to supervise closely whenever he is with the animal. Because watching a young child and a pet takes a lot of time and energy, many parents decide not to get a pet until their child is at least 5 years old. That way, the child will be old enough to take responsibility for some of the pet's care and will better understand how the pet should be handled.

CARETAKERS
AND PRESCHOOLS

How Can I Choose a Good Pediatrician?

Every family wants a pediatrician who is dependable, competent, caring, and easy to talk to. Some doctors are all of these things but others are not. Therefore, when parents are looking for a pediatrician, they should take the time to visit several doctors, seek recommendations, and ask questions. Because the family's relationship with its pediatrician will be a long and involved one, it is important that parents choose their child's doctor carefully.

To get the names of pediatricians you can interview, ask for recommendations from friends, relatives, or your obstetrician or midwife. You can also check with local hospitals and the referral services of local medical societies. Once you have the names of several pediatricians, set up appointments to visit. It is always best to see at least two doctors so you can compare them before you make your decision. Some doctors charge for consultations, so ask about fees.

When you visit each pediatrician's office, look around. Are there toys and books available for children? Is the floor clean enough for a baby to crawl on? Are sick and healthy children separated? Do the receptionists and nurses seem pleasant?

When you talk to the doctor, ask questions, and pay attention to how she responds. Does she answer you fully, in terms you can understand, and does she listen to your point of view? Do you feel comfortable with her? How do you think she relates to children?

Here are some of the questions you might want to ask during your interview: Will the pediatrician come to the hospital to examine your newborn? How does the pediatrician feel about breastfeeding and bottlefeeding, and does she approve of the feeding method you've chosen? Does she make herself available to discuss non-medical issues such as pacifier use, sleeping habits, and nutrition? Does she have regular call-in hours when you can ask questions over the phone? Is there a fee for phone consultations?

As you consider which pediatrician to use, think about such practical issues as the distance from the doctor's office to your home, the doctor's office hours (some pediatricians have extended hours for working parents), her fees, her procedure for emergency visits, and how her office handles insurance. If the doctor practices alone, find out who covers for her when she is sick or on vacation, and try to meet that doctor briefly. If the pediatrician you interview is part of a group practice, ask if you can choose one of the doctors as your primary pediatrician.

Choose a doctor you feel comfortable talking to, since you will frequently consult with her about your child's growth and development, and medical problems. You may find that after you start taking your child to a pediatrician, your feelings about that doctor will change. You may not have known, at the time you first interviewed her, that you would be facing such issues as pacifier use, sleep problems, late toilet use, etc. Now you discover that her opinions about these issues are contrary to yours. She may, for example, be against giving bottles to a toddler, while you think it is acceptable.

In such situations, some parents, who feel intimidated by their pediatrician, choose to hide their child's behavior when they come in for appointments. They leave their child's blanket, pacifier, or bottle at home, rather than face the doctor's disapproval. Such parents may eventually grow distant from their pediatrician, seeking her advice only on medical issues. Other parents in the same situation may become more open with their doctor, letting her know just how their child behaves and discussing differences of opinion on parenting issues. If you find yourself disagreeing with your child's doctor, you will have to decide whether to work out a compromise you can be satisfied with or switch pediatricians and start a new relationship.

I Need a Babysitter
I Can Trust

It can be difficult for parents to find a teenage babysitter they feel comfortable using. When parents leave their child for an afternoon or evening, they want to know that he will be happy and safe. Yet it is hard to tell from a quick conversation or a few minutes' observation whether a sitter will be responsible. The best way for parents to select a sitter is to ask for recommendations, get to know the sitter, and monitor carefully the way she performs the job.

To find potential sitters, ask friends, neighbors, relatives, and co-workers for recommendations. You can also ask local high school teachers or counselors for suggestions. Good sources of names are sitters who may be too busy to work for you but who can pass on names of friends who might babysit. Whatever your source for babysitters, get suggestions from people you trust, especially now when there is so much worry about potential child abuse. Also, as you seek referrals, keep in mind the ages of babysitters. Parents of infants may prefer an older teenager while parents of 4- and 5-year-olds may be happy with a 13- or 14-year-old sitter who will keep their child entertained.

After you have contacted a potential sitter, invite her to your home so you can meet her and observe her with your child. Ask questions about her activities, schoolwork, and friends. She will be pleased that you take an interest in her, and from her responses you will get to know what she is like. Watch as she interacts with your child. Is she friendly, playful, nurturing? How does your child respond to her? One father was delighted when the girl he was interviewing spontaneously took out her keys and jiggled them in front of his whimpering 18-month-old, calming the child. If the sitter is young or inexperienced, you may want to meet her parents—and they may want to meet you.

If you decide to use the sitter, have her arrive early on the day she will watch your child so you can give her instructions. Teenagers need strong guidance and limits, so be prepared to tell your sitter in detail what your expectations are. Describe how you want her to handle feeding, playtime, television, toilet use, and bedtime, and write down your instructions so she can refer to them later. Make it clear if you don't want her to talk on the phone, invite her friends to your house, or take your child outside.

Before you leave, let your sitter know how you can be reached and leave emergency phone numbers. You might also want to write down a list of activities your child enjoys, and another list of things to do (take out play dough, read books, etc.) if your child gets silly or hard to handle. A 4- or 5-year-old may spend time testing a new sitter and feeling a sense of power: "This is my house, my food, my TV." Let your child know ahead of time that you expect him to behave appropriately, and let your sitter know that it may take time for your child to feel comfortable with her.

If your young child has a difficult time separating from you, you might feel tempted to leave without warning him or saying goodbye. But if you do this, you will probably increase his anxiety. It is better to tell him you are going and have the sitter comfort him as you leave. If he will be asleep when you go, tell him before bedtime, "While you are sleeping, Linda will come and babysit for you." You can also take time before the babysitter arrives to tell your child about the fun he and the sitter will have. If you let the sitter do special things with your child—give an extra dessert, play a new game—your child may be less anxious about your leaving.

While you are out, you may want to call home to see how things are going. Occasionally, your sitter will tell you that your child is not feeling well and you will then have to cut your evening short. This can be frustrating, and at times upsetting. But it will happen less and less as your child gets older.

If you want to check on a relatively new sitter, come home a bit earlier than you told the sitter you would. And always ask how the afternoon or evening went. Since some sitters are reluctant to tell about problems or minor accidents, ask, "Any problems, scrapes, or bruises?"

Trust your instincts. If you feel that something happened while you were away, try to find out about it. If your child seems unhappy with a sitter, try to learn why. You can ask a 3- to 5-year-old, "What do you like about Michelle? What don't you like?" Although you may hear some exaggerated stories, you should take your child seriously when he says, "She yells too much." If you are unsure about a sitter, ask a neighbor to come by and check next time the sitter is at your house. And if you feel that a sitter is not responsible or is abusing your child in any way, stop using her and look for someone else. In order to enjoy your time away from home, you have to feel good about the person watching your child.

How Can I Choose the Best Nursery School or Day Care Center for My Child?

Every nursery school and day care center is different, and parents have to search carefully to find a good place for their child. Schools might claim (as Montessori, Waldorf, co-op, and religious schools do) that their programs are based on familiar philosophies, but parents have to see how the philosophies are actually implemented. The personalities of staff members, the physical layouts, and the day-to-day programs are what determine a school or center's quality. The only way for parents to make an informed choice is to observe a number of programs.

Parents who want a nursery school program that meets three mornings a week and parents searching for a day care center open 11 hours a day will be looking for the same qualities. All parents want caring staff members, a pleasant facility, and a flexible program that will meet their child's needs for the one to four years she will attend. The difference for parents looking at full-time day care is that their child will spend most of her waking hours at the center they choose. Therefore, the selection of a quality day care program is essential.

As you look for child care facilities, narrow your choices to centers that are easy to get to. If you are considering part-time nursery schools, you will probably want one close to home, while you might find a day care center more convenient if it is close to your work. Narrow your choices further by asking friends, neighbors, and co-workers for recommendations. Then visit at least two or three programs before making a decision.

When you go to a center or school, think about the physical space. Are the rooms inviting, clean, and safe? Is there ample room to play inside and is there play equipment outside? Are there places in the classroom where your child can play quietly? Are there a variety of toys and materials within easy reach? Where will your child take naps, and where can she go if she doesn't nap? Does the overall environment seem exciting?

Watch the teachers and aides carefully, since they set the tone for the program. Do they seem to enjoy their jobs and do they relate well to each other? Do you like the way they interact with the children? Good teachers will be warm and understanding, and respectful of children. Do the teachers seem reassuring and flexible enough to let a child follow her own interests? Are you comfortable with the way the teachers set limits and carry out discipline in the classroom?

Try to imagine your child in the programs you observe. How would she react? Are the teachers' expectations appropriate for her? Would the schedule allow her flexibility? What if she wanted to continue with one activity when the teachers had scheduled a switch to another—would she be allowed quietly to finish what she was doing?

See if the teachers pay enough attention to the children in the room. One parent saw a teacher, who was very involved with a small group working on the day's curriculum project, ignore the rest of the class. When the teacher finally became aware of an argument in the block corner, she was too late to help a child whose building had been destroyed.

Consider how many teachers there are at the center or school, and the makeup of the children's groups. Two-year-olds should be in a room with one adult for every four or five students. Children this young need a lot of attention and like to be held and comforted. Older children need fewer adults, but the teacher-child ratio should still seem satisfactory to you. Are there mixed age groups in a single classroom, or are children placed with others the same age? You may prefer one arrangement over another.

Pay particular attention to the school or center's program. Too many programs are highly structured and goal-oriented,

arranged with parents' and not children's needs in mind. Many teachers say, "Parents want academics. Parents expect projects." But when academics are over-emphasized, children lose opportunities to play, experiment with different materials, and come up with discoveries and their own answers to problems. In an effective program, children have plenty of time to explore on their own and teachers value active play and socializing.

Look at the children's artwork. Most nursery schools and centers have children do one or two art projects a day. Is the work displayed at a child's eye level? Are all the projects pre-cut by the teacher? Do all the finished projects look alike, or are they truly products of the children's effort and creativity?

Finally, see if the school or center's activities are appropriate for the children. One group of 2-year-olds was expected to dye Easter eggs in school, but the children were clearly incapable of following the necessary steps. Rather than drop the activity, the teachers did all the dyeing themselves.

Young children don't need to be introduced to activities they can't complete. Teachers should build on children's interests and abilities, not give them tasks they can't perform. Look for a program that stresses exploration and discovery and teachers who will follow up on your child's own interests and abilities.

What If I Don't Send Him
to Nursery School?

Parents feel pressure to send their child to nursery school since most children go and most child care professionals recommend it. Parents who keep their child home until elementary school often face the disapproval of friends and relatives. People ask, "How will he learn to socialize and relate to adults?" "Is something wrong with him? Isn't he ready?" "Aren't you afraid he'll miss out?" "How will he be prepared for kindergarten?"

There are a number of good reasons why a child might not go to nursery school. When there is a new baby in the family, some parents keep their older child home so he won't feel rejected or pushed out. The expense of nursery school deters other families, either because they can't afford the fees or don't think the experience is worth the cost. Some parents are unable to find a nursery school that seems appropriate for their child, and some parents want to be with their child full time until elementary school begins. Finally, some parents keep their child at home because they welcome the freedom: when there are no school schedules to follow, parent and child can wake up when they want, go on outings together, and stay outdoors as long as they like.

A child who stays out of nursery school will not be harmed socially. He will have chances to play with siblings, neighborhood children, and friends who attend part-time or half-day programs. His parents can also enroll him in once-a-week recreation classes and set up a visiting arrangement with other children who do not attend nursery school.

When a child goes to nursery school, his parents often marvel at how he changes. He seems more cooperative and knowledgeable, and they attribute his growth to the school. But parents whose children stay at home also see these changes. Young children naturally mature and develop as they get older, and a 4-year-old who stays home will have the same interest in learning and playing as a 4-year-old in a preschool.

A child who stays home will be busy and involved, especially if his parents provide an environment in which he can explore, play, and create. He will learn about his world because, like all young children, he is curious. Nursery school can be a very positive experience, but it isn't a necessary one.

If you decide to keep your child at home for the preschool years, you may wonder how he will adjust to kindergarten. As long as you prepare him by visiting the school ahead of time and talking about kindergarten activities, he will do just as well as a child who attended preschool. Kindergarten is a new experience for all children, and they all go through a period of adjustment.

During the years that your child is at home instead of in nursery school, people will often ask him, "Where do you go to school?" and his friends will tell him about their schools. Your child, particularly if he is 4 or 5, may wonder why he isn't in school, and may feel somewhat alienated from his friends. Many children, however, are not affected by the questions and comments of others, and confidently announce, "I don't go to school," or "I learn at home." If your child does express a desire to go to nursery school, you may want to look for a program that meets your needs as well as his, or you may decide to tell him that he will go to school when he is old enough for kindergarten.

Although the decision to keep your child home may be a

difficult one, you might be surprised by unexpected support. One mother, expecting a lecture, reluctantly told her pediatrician she was not sending her child to school. The doctor shocked and delighted her by not only praising her decision, but telling her that he too had kept his children home and that the experience had been very positive.

How Should I Prepare
My Child for Nursery School
or Day Care?

When a child begins nursery school or day care, she and her family face the issues of separation and independence. A 4- or 5-year-old will probably go off without much difficulty, but many children under 3 have a hard time leaving their parents. Parents can make the transition from home a little easier if they talk to their child about what will be happening, and patiently reassure her.

You can begin preparing your child several weeks before her new program starts. If she previously went with you to visit the school or center, remind her of what she saw: "Remember the blocks and puzzles you played with there?" If she has never seen the school, describe the building, the toys, and the activities. Let her know about snacks, lunch, and naps, and reassure her that the school has bathrooms and places for her coat and other belongings. Mention the name of someone she knows who will be in the program with her; if she doesn't know anyone in the school, tell her there will be many other children her age there. If you know who your child's teachers will be, tell her their names.

If your child is under 2, you won't be able fully to prepare her for nursery school or day care because she won't understand much of what you tell her, although you can still describe whatever you think will interest her. She will basically have to experience the new program, and the separation, firsthand. You and your child's caretakers will have to be understanding and nurturing as she adjusts in the early weeks of school, and you may have to be flexible about your own schedule so you can take your child home early if necessary.

On the first day of school, before you and your child leave home, talk to her about the separation that's coming: "After we get to the classroom, I'll stay for a few minutes and then say goodbye." Tell her what time you'll be coming back and what your driving arrangements will be. If she will be in a car pool, tell her who will drive. For the first few days of school you may want to do the driving yourself to help your child adjust to her new situation.

Be patient as you say goodbye to your child the first few days. Many children, especially those under 3 years old, have a difficult time leaving their parents, particularly if the program lasts a full day. Your child may want to say goodbye several times, or she may cry. Don't threaten her or say, "Be good and stop crying," or "Be a big girl." Your child needs support, not pressure. You might be able to eliminate some of your child's anxiety by letting her bring along a favorite toy or blanket. Try arriving at school 15 minutes early so you can spend more time with her before you go. Or give her a special little treat when she gets in the car or a "love" note or picture to carry into school with her.

You should not try to sneak out of the school without saying goodbye to your child, even if you think such an action might keep your child from crying. Eventually she will notice you are gone and may become frightened and upset. Although it is painful to see your child cry as you go, you should still say goodbye to her. You might feel better if you wait outside the classroom door, listening for a few minutes until she has calmed down.

If time goes by and your child continues to have trouble leaving you at the school door, consult with her teachers. They may be able to help by getting your child involved in activities as soon as she arrives. They may also tell you that your child cries for only a moment when you leave, and that you actually make her separation harder by staying extra minutes when you drop her off.

It might take your child several weeks to adjust to school, and during that time you may see some behavior changes: bedwetting, nightmares, decreased appetite, more frequent whining, and reluctance to go to school. Getting used to school is more difficult for some children than for others, but most children are affected in some way during the early days of a new program. You will have to be patient and understanding as your child adjusts.

If, after several months, your child is still showing behavior changes and seems unhappy in school, talk to her teachers and stay to observe the program. You might even drop in unexpectedly to see how your child is, and to try to find out why your child isn't enjoying herself. As you watch your child, ask yourself the following questions: Does she seem to have friends she enjoys? Is she one of the youngest children in the group? (If she is, she may feel less confident and accepted.) Is she getting enough attention from her teachers? If the program seems inappropriate for your child, consider taking her out of the school. But if you are unsure, wait before making your decision. Your child just might need an extra amount of understanding and time before she adjusts to day care or school.

I'm Having a Difficult Time Adjusting to Day Care

When parents work full-time outside the home they often send their child to a day care center. Yet 8 to 11 hours a day, five days a week is a long time for parents and children to be apart, and the separation usually takes an emotional toll on parents. They miss their child, particularly when he first begins a program, and worry about the care he is receiving. Is he happy? Safe? Are his teachers taking an interest in him? Does he have friends?

Parents may feel guilty because they fear that day care will have a negative effect on their child. If they see his behavior change, they wonder if it is because of his day care program. They feel bad about not spending enough time with him, and a mother, especially, may wonder whether she should have gone to work full-time in the first place. Even when parents and child are together in the evenings, the effects of work and day care continue. There is never enough time together at home and parents who want time to themselves feel guilty about not paying enough attention to their child, although he might actually enjoy playing alone after hours of sharing.

If you are concerned about having your child in a full-time program, your feelings are natural and shared by other parents in the same situation. There are things you can do to help yourself feel better and to solve some of the child care–related problems you experience. The most important step is to reassure yourself about your child's well-being by staying in close contact with his teachers. Call the center periodically during the day and find out how your child is doing. If the teachers agree (and they should), ask that your child be brought to the phone so you can talk to him. When you have a chance, drop by the center unannounced so you can observe him at play. You will immediately feel relieved if you see him happily involved.

If you suspect that your child is unhappy at his day care center, don't ignore the problem, even if you feel desperate about the need for child care. It takes a great deal of effort and energy to become involved in your child's day care situation; some parents avoid or deny all problems because they don't have the time or energy to cope. Other parents are afraid even to question their child about his day, for fear he will say something negative.

If you are worried about your child's adjustment to day care, you have to take the responsibility of investigating and becoming involved enough to help him. You may find support and good ideas if you ask other parents how they solved their day care problems. And you may discover that once you start communicating openly with your child's teachers, his situation will improve and you and he will feel better about his full day away from home.

When Should My Child Learn ABCs and Numbers?

Many preschool and day care programs claim to be "academic," teaching very young children to count, recite the alphabet, and learn various concepts. Such emphasis on educational activities is part of a larger, society-wide push to have children learn more, faster. Publishers put out educational books and materials; toy companies manufacture educational games; television shows such as "Sesame Street" teach the alphabet and numbers. Because of pressure from friends, neighbors, some child development professionals, and the media, many parents feel concerned if their 2- or 3- or 4-year-old hasn't yet learned shapes, colors, and numbers.

It is possible to teach a young child to memorize and then recite back almost any short list, including the numbers from 1 to 10 and the alphabet. But comprehension of abstract concepts doesn't usually begin until the child is 4 to 6 years old. A 3-year-old may know that saying "1, 2, 3, 4," is called counting, but she probably will not understand that the number 6 represents six objects. And to a young child, learning the alphabet is like learning to recite in a foreign language without knowing the meaning of the words.

A child can't be taught to understand concepts before she is ready. Gradually, as she experiments with objects, questions her parents and other people, observes her environment, and explores, she will learn what words and numbers mean. If her natural curiosity is encouraged, and if she has materials to experiment with, she will learn concepts easily. But if parents coach their child and put too much emphasis on her early education, they may discourage her and diminish her natural drive to learn. Parents should wait until their child shows a spontaneous interest in letters, words, and concepts, then follow up on what she can do.

There is no need for schools and parents to provide excessive amounts of educational materials for young children. Colors, shapes, numbers, and letters are part of whatever children do, so children learn about these things naturally. Every day, a child hears, "Put on your blue shorts," "Do you want the red or the green crayon?" "Here are three crackers," "Look at that big truck." The child has constant exposure to such concepts as same and different (milk is different from juice, Mom is different from Dad), soft and hard, big and little, etc. She hears adults counting, sees them reading, and observes letters and numbers everywhere.

Because your child learns everywhere, there is no need to formally teach her numbers and letters. You will gradually see her take an interest and hear her ask, "How many is this?" "What color is this?" She will begin to count out loud, at first getting the numbers out of order, and she will write letters on paper, often creating nonsense words or writing her name backwards. Try not to correct her, but rather encourage her to keep counting and keep writing. She will learn what she needs to know, and she will learn it because she is self-motivated, not because you or her teachers are pressuring her to learn fast.

What Should I Look For in Recreation Classes?

Parents enroll their child in community recreation classes so he can pick up new skills and enjoy himself. Sometimes these classes arc well-run and satisfying, but at other times they are poorly taught and disappointing. In order to choose classes wisely, parents should observe programs before registering and consider which activities are most appropriate for their child. Then, once class sessions begin, parents should monitor the program and help their child adjust to the teacher and the activities.

Before you sign up for a class, watch a session taught by the instructor your child will have. Although it may be difficult for you to arrange an observation, it is worth the effort. Many recreation programs sound exciting when described in catalogs and brochures, but turn out to be poorly run or inappropriate. If possible, take your child along so he can let you know if he is interested in the class.

As you watch a class session, ask yourself these questions: How structured is the program? Does it look like fun? Do the children seem to be enjoying themselves? How does the instructor respond to a child who is hesitant about joining the group? Is there unnecessary pressure on children to conform and achieve? Does the teacher seem to nurture creativity? Does the teacher say, "I like the way you did that," rather than "You can do better than that"? Does the teacher accept a child's limitations? How large is the class? Do children get a chance to show the teacher what they can do? Do they have to spend much time waiting for turns at the activities?

If, after observing, you decide to enroll your child in a class, briefly prepare him for the first session. Talk to him about the instructors, the equipment, the clothes he will wear, and any friends who will be in the class. Let him know about transportation arrangements and where you will be while the class meets. And since most children worry about the availability of bathrooms, reassure him that the recreation program has bathrooms.

On the first day of class, you will notice that some children quickly join in the activities while other children have difficulty adjusting. If your child is reluctant to get involved, you might feel discouraged and embarrassed, especially if the other class members are having an easy time. You might also feel alone, questioning your parenting abilities and wondering what you have done to make your child shy and unwilling to participate. You might also feel angry at your child, particularly if it was his idea to take the recreation class.

In such a situation, a supportive teacher can make you and your child feel better by smiling, waving, coming over to talk, and generally letting your child know he is accepted even if he doesn't choose to participate right away. You will also feel more comfortable if the other parents in the group are supportive rather than judgmental. While you are encouraging your child to participate, try not to pressure him to take part in the activities but rather accept his feelings and, if necessary, sit with him until he is comfortable enough to join the group.

In later class sessions, your child may continue to resist joining in or may become disenchanted with the program. Perhaps the instructor overwhelms your child, the other children seem too big, your child is not ready to separate from you, the teachers' (or your) expectations create too much pressure, your child is unwilling to join in because you are watching, or the class is not what your child thought it would be. He may have had his own fantasies about the program, imagining he would be free to jump on the trampoline, do somersaults, or improvise his own craft projects. But most programs allow little freedom—children are told what to do and how to do it, and they spend a lot of time waiting for their turns.

It is not unusual for a child's interest in a recreation program to dwindle as the weeks go by. You may hear, "I'll go another day," or "I don't want to go." Often, because of rigid structure or intense competition, the classes stop being fun. Think back on your own experience with recreation programs. The classes that you enjoyed and continued to attend were ones that provided fun, acceptance, and positive feedback. The ones you disliked made you feel unaccepted and pressured.

If your child wants to drop out of a recreation class, discuss the situation with the instructors. They can help you decide whether you should spend several sessions in the class, helping your child adjust, or whether he should stop attending. Don't force him to continue in a class he is not enjoying, since such pressure is likely to increase his resistance to all classes. If you are matter-of-fact about having your child quit a program, he will also accept the experience lightly and will probably not resist trying other classes in the future.

Is My Child Ready for Kindergarten?

As a child approaches the end of his preschool years, his parents begin to consider his readiness for kindergarten. Some parents confidently envision their child in kindergarten, but others, particularly those whose children have mid- to late-in-the-year birthdays, wonder if their child is ready for this major step. There are school districts that require children with late birthdays to wait an extra year before starting kindergarten, but most districts let parents choose whether to enroll their child during his 5th or 6th year. Because a child's success in the first year of school lays the foundation for later success, the decision to send a child to kindergarten must be made carefully and in the child's best interests.

Parents sometimes assume that a child who has been to nursery school is automatically prepared for kindergarten, but kindergarten is a different experience in a number of ways. Children in kindergarten are expected to spend scheduled amounts of time sitting and working on specific academic skill-building tasks. Although play is considered part of the daily program, emphasis is placed on group and individual academic work and on following a set curriculum. Kindergartners become part of a large school community that operates under new rules and expectations. And children find that their parents, who are excited about kindergarten, may begin to put emphasis on "doing well."

Although chronological age is the major factor determining kindergarten readiness, there naturally are related factors parents should consider: cognitive or intellectual development, social and emotional development, and physical size. If a child is 5 to 9 months younger than other kindergartners, he may display behavior that is significantly different from his classmates'. Even if he is advanced in one area of development, such as academics, he may generally be functioning at a level lower than expected for his age group.

To evaluate overall readiness for kindergarten, parents should first look at their child's cognitive development. When a child is functioning academically below kindergarten level, he can sometimes be helped through individualized instruction from teachers and specialists. But the child who is lagging behind often has a hard time catching up because learning in certain areas is too difficult for him. Despite the instructional support, the child might think he is "not as good" as his peers, and he may feel unnecessary stress because he cannot cope with the demands of school. When this happens, he will probably show signs of disliking school, say he hates school, or become a behavior problem.

Another area of concern to parents should be their child's social and emotional development. A child who is socially or emotionally immature may have a difficult time accommodating to his teacher's demands. He may seem unwilling to behave as kindergartners should, when actually he is unable to act more maturely. He may have a hard time working and playing cooperatively with his classmates and this may cause him to be labeled a "behavior problem." Naturally, if a child is labeled this way, his self-image will be affected, and ultimately, he will continue misbehaving because he feels frustrated and angry over his inability to do what is expected of him.

A child who lags behind socially but is advanced academically poses a dilemma for his parents, who may be concerned about holding him back an extra year. Parents may think their child will not be challenged in academic areas if he waits and attends kindergarten with younger children, yet, if the imbalance between social and intellectual development is striking, the child is probably not developmentally ready for kindergarten.

Another factor parents should consider is size and physical development. When a child is several months younger than the average kindergarten student, he may also be smaller than his classmates. Size and age are important to young children, who frequently check each other to see who is tallest and who is oldest. And since children often begin to lose their teeth during the kindergarten year, a younger child might be frustrated and unhappy if he doesn't lose teeth when his older friends do. Being the youngest and smallest can put a child in a vulnerable position in the classroom, although this would naturally be more of a problem for a child who is reserved and quiet rather than boisterous and outgoing.

If you are unsure about your child's readiness for kindergarten, seek opinions from others, including professionals. If your child has been to nursery school, the first people you contact will probably be your child's teachers. Since they have a basic understanding of kindergarten requirements and have had many opportunities to observe children, they will be able to advise you. As long as you like and trust them, their judgment may be very helpful. If you continue to have questions, seek the opinion of a developmental therapist who specializes in school readiness assessments. Your pediatrician may also be of help and may listen to your thoughts and concerns. Friends who have held their children back a year will probably be willing to share their thoughts with you, and elementary school counselors or principals will discuss the issue and offer information on kindergarten readiness.

Most parents who have held their children back a year have

not regretted the extra time for growing and maturing. The child who starts kindergarten when he is developmentally ready is better able to meet academic demands and get along with others. When children do not have to struggle to keep up, they develop a strong sense of self-confidence, and this provides a good start for the school years.

FOR THE BEST IN PAPERBACKS, LOOK FOR THE 🐧

In every corner of the world, on every subject under the sun, Penguin represents quality and variety—the very best in publishing today.

For complete information about books available from Penguin—including Pelicans, Puffins, Peregrines, and Penguin Classics—and how to order them, write to us at the appropriate address below. Please note that for copyright reasons the selection of books varies from country to country.

In the United Kingdom: For a complete list of books available from Penguin in the U.K., please write to *Dept E.P., Penguin Books Ltd, Harmondsworth, Middlesex, UB7 0DA*.

In the United States: For a complete list of books available from Penguin in the U.S., please write to *Consumer Sales, Penguin USA, P.O. Box 999— Dept. 17109, Bergenfield, New Jersey 07621-0120*. VISA and MasterCard holders call 1-800-253-6476 to order all Penguin titles.

In Canada: For a complete list of books available from Penguin in Canada, please write to *Penguin Books Canada Ltd, 10 Alcorn Avenue, Suite 300, Toronto, Ontario, Canada M4V 3B2*.

In Australia: For a complete list of books available from Penguin in Australia, please write to the *Marketing Department, Penguin Books Ltd, P.O. Box 257, Ringwood, Victoria 3134*.

In New Zealand: For a complete list of books available from Penguin in New Zealand, please write to the *Marketing Department, Penguin Books (NZ) Ltd, Private Bag, Takapuna, Auckland 9*.

In India: For a complete list of books available from Penguin, please write to *Penguin Overseas Ltd, 706 Eros Apartments, 56 Nehru Place, New Delhi, 110019*.

In Holland: For a complete list of books available from Penguin in Holland, please write to *Penguin Books Nederland B.V., Postbus 195, NL-1380AD Weesp, Netherlands*.

In Germany: For a complete list of books available from Penguin, please write to *Penguin Books Ltd, Friedrichstrasse 10-12, D-6000 Frankfurt Main 1, Federal Republic of Germany*.

In Spain: For a complete list of books available from Penguin in Spain, please write to *Longman, Penguin España, Calle San Nicolas 15, E-28013 Madrid, Spain*.

In Japan: For a complete list of books available from Penguin in Japan, please write to *Longman Penguin Japan Co Ltd, Yamaguchi Building, 2-12-9 Kanda Jimbocho, Chiyoda-Ku, Tokyo 101, Japan*.